# DANTE
# BEYOND THE *COMMEDIA*

*Edited with a Preface by* Anne Paolucci

### Dante Alighieri
### *A QUESTION OF THE WATER AND OF THE LAND*
*Translated with a Introduction by*
Charles Hamilton Bromby

### *DANTE'S INFLUENCE ON AMERICAN WRITERS 1776-1976*
*Edited with an Introduction by*
Anne Paolucci
*Opening Remarks by*
Hon. Alessandro Cortese DeBosis,
Hon. Lester Wolff, Hon. Mario Biaggi
*Articles by*
J. Chesley Mathews, James J. Wilhelm,
And Glauco Cambon

### Anne Paolucci / Henry Paolucci
### *DANTE AND THE "QUEST FOR ELOQUENCE" IN INDIA'S VERNACULAR LANGUAGES*

Copyright © 2004 by Anne Paolucci

Library of Congress Cataloging-in-Publication Data

Dante : beyond the Commedia / edited wuth a preface by Anne Paolucci.
   p. cm.
   Includes bibliographical references.
   Contents: Question of the water and of the land /Dante Alighieri ; translated by Charles Hamilton Bromby – Dante's influence on American writers, 1776-1976 / J. Chesley Mathews, James J. Wilhelm, Glauco Cambon – Dante and the "quest for eloquence" in India's vernacular languages / Anne Paolucci/ Henry Paolucci.
   ISBN 1-932107-09-6 (alk. paper)
   1. Dante Alighieri, 1265-1321—Influence. 2. American literature—Italian influences. 3. Indian literature—Italian influences. I. Bromby, Charles Hamilton, 1843-1904. II. Paolucci, Anne. III. Dante Alighieri, 1265-1321. Quaestio de aqua et terra. English. IV. Mathews, Joseph Chesley, 1906- Dante's influece on American writers, 1776-1976. V. Paolucci, Anne. Dante and the "quest for eloquence in India's vernacular languages.

PQ4335.D29 2004
851'.1—dc22
                                            2003056888

---

*Published by*
**GRIFFON HOUSE PUBLICATIONS**
*for*
**THE BAGEHOT COUNCIL**
**P. O. BOX 30727**
**WILMINGTON, DE, 19805-7727**
griffonhse@AOL.com

## CONTENTS

*Preface* (ANNE PAOLUCCI)   v

### PART ONE (pp. 1-32)
*A QUESTION OF THE WATER AND OF THE LAND*
BY DANTE ALIGHIERI
(Translated by Charles Hamilton Bromby)

| | |
|---|---:|
| *Translator's Introduction* | 3 |
| Question | 9 |
| First Reason | 10 |
| Second Reason | 10 |
| Third Reason | 11 |
| Fourth Reason | 11 |
| Fifth Reason | 11 |
| Order of the Question | 12 |
| Determination in Two Modes | 12 |
| First and Second Supposition | 13 |
| Destruction of the First Member | 13 |
| Destruction of the Second Member | 15 |
| He concludes that the Water is Concentric | 16 |
| He argues Contra; and first | 16 |
| He argues against the Things that have been Determined | 17 |
| The preceding Reason is met by an Objection | 18 |
| The Objection is Answered | 19 |
| Of the Efficient Cause of the Elevation of the Land | 22 |
| *Notes* | 28 |

## PART TWO (pp. 33-71)
### *DANTE'S INFLUENCE ON AMERICAN WRITERS 1776-1976*
(Edited with an Introduction by Anne Paolucci)

| | |
|---|---:|
| *Introduction* (ANNE PAOLUCCI) | 35 |
| Opening Remarks | |
|     The Honorable Alessandro Cortese DeBosis, Consul General of Italy in New York | 37 |
| Greetings | |
|     The Honorable Lester Wolff, House of Representatives, 6th[th] District, New York | 39 |
| Greetings | |
|     The Honorable Mario Biaggi, House of Representatives, 10th District, New York | 41 |
| Historical Overview of American Writers Interest in Dante (to About 1900) (J. Chesley Mathews) | 42 |
| Two Visions of the Journey of Life: Dante as Guide for Eliot and Pound (James J. Wilhelm) | 53 |
| Dante on Galway Kinnell's "Last River" (Glauco Cambon) | 62 |

## PART THREE (pp. 73-166)
### *DANTE AND THE "QUEST FOR ELOQUENCE" IN INDIA'S VERNACULAR LANGUAGES*
(Anne Paolucci / Henry Paolucci)

| | |
|---|---:|
| *Introduction* | 75 |
| 1. The Sanskrit Revival: From Comparative Linguistics to Classical Nostalgia | 81 |
| 2. Bengali's Development on the Latin-Italian Model | 98 |
| 3. Gandhi and the Linguistic Surveys of Dante, Grierson and S. K. Chatterji | 128 |
| 4. Conclusion: Literary India Today | 156 |
| *Notes* | 160 |

# PREFACE

The three Parts of this volume represent scattered materials that deal with some lesser known aspects of Dante's work. They are interesting, of course, for their connection with Dante but also claim attention in scientific and comparative fields of study.

"Part One," *A Question of the Water and of the Land*, appeared in English for the first time in a small volume published by David Nutt (London, 1897), in the translation of Charles Hamilton Bromby. In his Introduction, Bromby touches on the ongoing controversy about authorship, defending the authenticity of the work ("it breaths of Dante throughout" [p. 28, n. 1]) and refers the reader to Moore's *Studies in Dante* for more on the subject. He cannot resist mentioning, however — in order to quickly discredit Scar-tazzini's argument against authenticity: that Dante could not have written the short treatise since "the idea of the tides being caused by the moon was undreamt of in Dante's day." [p. 28, n.1]. Bromby counters by noting that not only was Dante "in many ways . . . before his age" and therefore quite capable of having anticipated others in this inquiry, but that the theory put forward, as Paget Toynbee points out in an article published in *Romania* (July, 1895), was known in fact as far back as Albertus Magnus (d. 1280), who mentions it. (p. 8, n.) Certainly the work deserves to be made accessible again, for both readers of Dante and anyone interested in its scientific implications.

"Part Two" was first conceived in the early 1970s, when I was Vice-President of The Dante Society of America. At one of the Board meetings, held at Harvard (the great center of Dante studies in the early 1800s and still the home of the Society), I suggested that we plan some special projects for the bicentennial year. The Board agreed; and when asked for ideas, I put forward two possibilities, both of which were accepted. One was a collection of essays by eminent American Danteists like the renowned Dino Bigongiari, who — among others — taught a graduate course on "Dante and Medieval Culture" in the English and Comparative Literature Department of Columbia University for a number of years — a course in which I was privileged to take part. Bart Giarnatti, who later became President of Yale, was then President of the Society and volunteered to take on this project. The collection was assembled and published some time later.

The second idea was to plan a special bicentenial meeting of the Society at the annual convention of the Modern Language Association of America, which in 1976 was held in New York, I chose as our topic "Dante's Influence on American Writers: 1776-1976" and recruited three excellent speakers J. Chesley Mathews, James J. Wilhelm, and poet-critic Glauco Cambon — as well as the Consul General of Italy in New York, Dr. Alessandro Cortese DeBosis, and Congressmen Lester Wolff and Mario Biaggi for some preliminary remarks. The program drew a record crowd (for an "Affiliated Organization" of MLA) of over 300 people. The entire program was made accessible in a small pamphlet the next year and has been reproduced here in its entirety, as "Part Two."

The final section of the present volume, "Part Three," makes available again a long article first written for the India volume of *Review of National Literatures* (vol. 10, 1979, pp, 70-144; Special Editor Ronald Warwick [a specialist in South Asian literatures, who was with the Commonwealth Institute in London). The article, "Dante and 'The Quest for Eloquence' in India's Vernacular Languages," received a great deal of attention, at the time, both here and in India, where it was hailed in major reviews as the first study of its kind, In it, Professor Henry Paolucci and I traced the interesting correspondences between the languages of India and those of the Italian city-states and regions of Dante's time, which the great poet examined and described, in *De Vulgari Eloquentia*, in his effort to promote a single language that would serve the entire Italian peninsula.

Much else might have been included here; but the writings chosen, if not unique, proved an excellent representative sampling of areas "beyond the *Commedia*," where Dante can be studied profitably. Toward that end they have been brought together and made available again in the present volume.

*ANNE PAOLUCCI*
February, 2004

A

# QUESTION OF THE WATER AND OF THE LAND

BY

DANTE ALIGHIERI

*TRANSLATED INTO ENGLISH, WITH AN INTRODUCTION AND NOTES BY*

CHARLES HAMILTON BROMBY

LONDON
DAVID NUTT, 270–271, STRAND
1897

# PART ONE

*A QUESTION OF THE WATER
AND OF THE LAND*
by
DANTE ALIGHIERI

(TRANSLATED BY CHARLES HAMILTON BROMBY)

TRANSLATOR'S INTRODUCTION

My apology for making a translation of this treatise into English is that no one else has done it. Of all the authentic works of Dante this alone remains untranslated. Professor Longhena, many years ago, translated it into Italian; besides that, I know of no one else who has put it into any modern language. And yet it has a peculiar interest apart from the fact that it is undoubtedly authentic.[1] It is Dante's latest work, written a year before his death, and probably after the Paradiso was completed. It is interesting, too, as the only work of the kind we have from him, and it shows him in a new light, taking a part in the scientific discussions of the day. It is also most interesting as a specimen of the class of questions which were discussed then, and the manner of dealing with them. It is a good example of the intellectual exercises, or tournaments, in which men of intelligence and learning delighted at that time. And though it was not, perhaps, intended as a very serious question, it is handled with all the seriousness of his grave nature, and is written in his most argumentative style. The excuse for writing it, that his enemies might not speak untruthfully of his views on the subject behind his back, and the bitter, if half humorous, sarcasm at the end, on those who would not come to hear the discourse, is typical of Dante.

I have ventured to add some notes of explanation and reference, but I have not attempted anything like a commentary. To attempt a commentary would require more time and space than I am prepared to give, and I shrink from being the first to endeavor to explain some of the reasonings and expressions which I confess seem to me obscure and difficult.

To understand Dante's conception of the universe

it is necessary to know something of the theories of the world and its surroundings as held by the principal astronomers among the ancients: Aristotle, Hipparchus, Ptolemy. Ptolemy, indeed, did little beyond enlarging on the teaching of Hipparchus, and drawing his conclusions from that other's observations.[2] Hipparchus was, perhaps, the greatest astronomical genius, considering his want of instruments, and the paucity of previous observations, that the world has produced. At Dante's time little progress had been made in the twelve hundred years since Ptolemy made his calculations.

The idea of the universe through all that time, and for a long while before and after it, was a great transparent hollow ball, with a geometric or imaginary line, running from its most northern to its southern point, or pole,[3] round which imaginary axis the great hollow ball, or sphere, revolved. In the sides of this sphere, which was called the eighth heaven, or the heaven of the stars, the fixed stars were fastened. These stars were also believed to be balls or spheres. In the space inside the large ball came a number of other spheres, all revolving round the imaginary line. First came the sphere of Saturn in which that planet was placed, and which carried the planet round with its own peculiar motion, and was called the seventh heaven, or heaven of Saturn.[4] Next came Jupiter in its sphere under similar conditions, the sixth or heaven of Jupiter. Next after Jupiter came Mars in the same way, called the fifth heaven or heaven of Mars; and then the Sun, which was also supposed to be a planet, in its heaven, the fourth. Between the Sun and the Earth were Venus, Mercury, and the Moon, each giving its name to its own heaven, the third, second, and first respectively. The three planets above the Sun — *i.e.*, Saturn, Jupiter, Mars, were called the superior planets; Venus and Mercury between the Sun and the Moon, the inferior.

Such were the old conceptions of the surrounding heavens. The earliest men of science thought of them, and believed in them, as they appeared to them to be. But philosophers required something more. What made all these spheres to move? Ptolemy answered this by imagining an exciting energy outside the eighth or starry heaven, and which in Dante's time was known as the Primum Mobile, or ninth heaven — an active sphere moving from east to west giving force or motion to all the other spheres.

This was not sufficient for Christian philosophers. They accepted the Primum Mobile as giving force or motion to the other heavens, but beyond that again they taught there was a tenth heaven, the Empyreum, emphatically the abode of the Almighty and His angels, although in some way the other lower heavens, according to Dante at least, were indeed portions of the heaven of heavens.[5]

In the centre of this system came the earth. What the precise idea of the form of the earth was in Dante's time is doubtful.[6] Some seem to imagine that it was supposed to be a flat circular surface like a round table. This could not have been so, at any rate to the more learned of his day. Aristotle, Hipparchus and Ptolemy, had taught that the earth was a sphere, transfixed by the great pole which ran through the universe. But whatever they imagined the shape of the earth to be, its most learned inhabitants, in the Middle Ages, had no certain knowledge of any land beyond that of which they had experience themselves, had heard of from travelers, or were told about by the few great authorities they so implicitly trusted. In Dante's time the Pillars of Hercules, close to where Gibraltar now is, was its western boundary, India its boundary on the east, because Orosius, who was contemporary with St. Augustine, said so. Their knowledge of northern countries was vague and indistinct, and a short way towards the equator in Africa soon brought them to the extreme habitable south.[7] Round this limited portion of land they imagined a great circular ocean to roll, called poetically here "Amphitrite." Beyond this ocean came a space large enough to allow the sphere of the fixed stars to revolve. For they believed that these stars with the sphere in which they were placed revolved round the earth, with a regular motion, once in every twenty-four hours.[8] The sun had its own motion in its sphere. In the earliest times it was believed to sink into the western ocean every night, and the people of Gades, the modern Cadiz, the most western inhabitants of the earth, declared they could hear the great hissing it made as it entered the water, so imaginative were they, or the poet who related this of them.

Both Heraclitus and Pythagoras had held that the earth revolved on its axis, but Aristotle and Ptolemy denied this, and said it was utterly impossible. Dante, of course, followed Aristotle. It would have seemed to him a scientific heresy to doubt Aristotle on such a point. A remarkable thing is that, far as the ancient and medieval astronomers were from the truth, yet, as Sir G. C. Lewis points out in his *Astronomy of the Ancients*, for all practical purposes their system was as good as ours.

Besides Mr. Paget Toynbee's instructive article in *Romania*, I have made frequent use of Dr. Moore's learned and laborious work, *Studies in Dante*. But I do not understand the references of the latter to Aristotle's *De Mundo*. The treatise which goes by that title is spurious and of a later date. It has been pointed out to me that Simplicius in his commentary on the De Coelo," says, "Περὶ οὐρανοῦ Ἀριστοτέλους πραγματείας ὁ ΑλέΣανδρος περὶ κόσμου φήσιν"; this may account for Dante's calling the *De Coelo* the *De Coelo et Mundo*.

I have used the text of Fraticelli, corrected, since this translation was made, here and there by the recent Oxford edition, to whose editor all students of Dante are under an unspeakable obligation, and the Oxford edition of Bekker's *Aristotle* of 1837.

NOTES

1. I need not trouble the reader with all the arguments for and against the authenticity of the work. It breathes of Dante throughout. It seems, indeed, far more probable that Dante did write it, than

## Translator's Introduction

that any one should have caught his style so closely, should not only have searched through his authorities with a care altogether out of proportion to any possible gain to be got by the perpetration of a forgery, and should have shown the same peculiarities in his quotation of many of those authorities. For some of these "undesigned coincidences" I may refer the reader to Dr. Moore's *Studies in Dante*, especially pp, 105, 106.

As an example of the reasons given against its authenticity I may give one of Scartazzini's — that the idea of the tides being caused by the moon was undreamt of in Dante's day. Even if it was true that such a theory had not been known before Dante's time, it does not follow that the *Quæstio* is not a work of his, who in many ways was before his age. But, in fact, as is pointed out by Mr. Paget Toynbee, in his interesting article, published in a French magazine called *Romania*, in July 1895, the theory was known before Dante's time, and is mentioned by Albertus Magnus, who died in 1280, and who, when speaking of the moon, says, "*ideo mare et omne humidum movet ex seipsa*" (Tract I, cap.2).

2. *Le plus célèbre, sans contredit, mais non le plus veritablement grand astronome de toute l'antiquité. Nul n'a été loué avec plus d'exageration* (Delambre).

3. The Greek word πόλος, from which we get "pole," originally meant a ball, and was at first used to designate the cavity of the heavens as it is seen from the earth. So it came to mean a hemisphere, thence it was applied to the basin in which the earliest sundials were made, then to the central point in the hemisphere, or apex of the celestial sphere, with a line drawn from that apex through all the other spheres, and on to the central point in the Antarctic Circle (see Sir G. C. Lewis' *Astronomy of the Ancients*). In the fourth chapter of the second book of the *Convito*, Dante says that each heaven *di sotto del Cristallino*, has two poles, *poli fermi quanto a se*, while the ninth, the Crystalline heaven, or *Primum Mobile*, has them, *firmi e fissi e non mutabili secondo alcuno rispetto* — i.e., as regards any other thing.

4. I leave out of this necessarily slight sketch the complicated system of many several spheres, and epicycles, assigned to the planets by Aristotle and other ancient astronomers, by which they attempted to account for the irregular movements of the planets.

5. Dante gives his own peculiar and beautiful reason for the exceeding great and incomprehensible swiftness of the ninth heav-

en, the *Primum Mobile*, in its intense desire, *ferventissimo appetito*, to become one with the highest heaven, *quello divinissimo cielo quieto*, quiet and at peace because it has all its desire, *lo luogo di somma Deita*. (*Con.* II. iv.) The heaven of the peace divine (*Par.* ii. 112, and *Ep.* to *Can Grande*, p. 24, 25).

6. In the *Convito* (II. vii.) Dante shows that he not only knew the earth was a sphere, but that he was not so very far off its actual size, namely that it was 3250 miles to the centre of it. In *Con.* IV. viii. he gives 6500 miles as its diameter.

7. But in the *De Monarchia*, Dante speaks of a people called the Garamantes, who dwell beneath the equinoctial, and ever have the light of day equal to the shades of night. And in the *Convito*, (III. v. 170), *Garamanti . . . come detto è, in su questa palla veggia il sole appunto sopra sè girare.*

8. Dante gives the exact time of the revolution of the *Primum Mobile* as twenty-three hours and fourteen-fifteenths, *grossamente assegnando* (*Con.* II. iii.)

A GOLDEN AND MOST USEFUL QUESTION PROPOSED BY
DANTE ALAGHERIUS, THE RENOWNED FLORENTINE POET,
CONCERNING THE NATURE OF THE TWOFOLD ELEMENTS,
WATER AND LAND[1].

To all and singular who shall see these presents, Dantes Aligherius of Florence, least amongst true philosophers, health in Him who is the Prince and Light of Truth.

§ i. Let it be known to you all that while I was at Mantua a certain question arose, which though often dilated upon, for show rather than for the sake of truth, remained still undetermined. Wherefore I, who have been from my childhood continually nurtured in the love of truth, could not bear to leave the said question unexamined, but it pleased me to show the truth about this matter, and to refute the arguments upon the other side, as well from love of the truth as from hatred of falseness. And lest the malice of many, who are wont to fabricate lies against the absent who are the objects of their spite, should behind my back alter those things which have been well said, I have desired to leave written by my fingers on this folio that which has been determined by me, and to show forth with the pen the form of the whole disputation.

*Question.*
§ ii. The question then was about the local position and figure, or form, of the two elements, to wit, of the water and of the land. And I mean here by form, that which the philosopher places in the fourth species of quality in the predicaments.[2] And the question was restricted to this, so that at the beginning of investigating the truth it might be sought out — whether the water in its sphere, that is, in

its natural circumference, may be in any part higher than the land, which rises out of the water, and which we commonly call the habitable quarter; and it was argued that it did so for many reasons, of which some having been passed over on account of their foolishness, I have retained five, which seem to have some weight.

*First Reason.*

§ iii. The first was this: It is impossible that two circumferences unequally distant from one another can have the same centre; the circumference of the water and the circumference of the land are unequally distant; therefore, &c. Then it went on: since the centre of the land is the centre of the universe[3], as is affirmed by all, and everything that has a position in the world different to it[4] is higher, it was concluded that the circumference of the water is higher than the circumference of the land since the circumference follows everywhere the centre itself. The major of the principal syllogism is seen to be manifest through those things which are demonstrated in geometry, the minor through the senses, inasmuch as we see in some parts the circumference of the land to be included in the circumference of the water, in some parts to be excluded.

*Second Reason*

§ iv. To the more noble body a more noble place is due;[5] water is a more noble body than the land, therefore the more noble place is due to the water. And since a place is the more noble in so much as it is higher, because of its being nearer to the most noble continent, which is the first heaven;[6] therefore, &c. I pass by that the locality of the water is higher than the locality of the land, and consequently that the water is higher than the land, since the situation of the place and of the thing placed does not differ. The major and minor of the principal syllogism of this reason were dismissed as if manifest.[7]

## Third Reason

§ v. The third reason was: Every opinion which is contradictory to sense is a bad opinion; to be of opinion that the water is not higher than the land is to be contradictory to sense; therefore it is a bad opinion. The first was declared to be evident by the commentator in the third book *De Anima*[8]; the second, or minor, by the experience of sailors who behold, when at sea, the mountains beneath them; and they prove it by saying that by going up the mast they see them, while from the deck they do not see them; which seems to happen from this, that the land is much lower and deeper down than the ridge of the sea.

## Fourth Reason.

§ vi. Fourthly, it was thus argued: If the land was not lower than the water, the land would be altogether without water, at least in the uncovered part, about which we are inquiring; and so there would be neither fountains, nor rivers, nor lakes, of which fact we see the opposite; wherefore the opposite, which followed from that, is true, that the water is higher than the land. The consequence is proved by this that water is naturally brought down from above; and since the sea is the principle of all waters (as is shown by the philosopher in his treatise on Meteors[9]), if the sea was not higher than the land, the water would not be moved towards the earth, since that in natural motion the principle of the water must be higher.[10]

## Fifth Reason.

§ vii. Also it was argued fifthly: the water is seen particularly to follow the motion of the moon, as is shown in the ebb and flow of the sea; and since the orb of the moon is excentric,[11] it seems reasonable that the water in its sphere should imitate the excentricity of the orb of the moon, and consequently be excentric; and since this could not be unless it was higher than the earth, as was shown in the first reason, the same conclusion follows as before.

§ viii. By these reasons, therefore, and others we need not care about, those endeavour to show that their opinion is true who hold that the water is higher than that portion of the land which is uncovered, or habitable, however much sense and reason is against it. For as to sense, we see throughout the whole land, as well south as north, as well east as west, the rivers descend to the sea; which would not be if the source of the rivers, and the course of their beds, were not higher than this level of the sea. As to reason, it will appear further on; and this will be demonstrated by many proofs in showing or determining the position and form of the two elements, as was touched upon above.

## Order of the Question

§ ix. This will be the order. First, it will be demonstrated that it is impossible that the water in any part of its circumference is higher than the land which emerges from it, or lies uncovered by it. Secondly, it will be demonstrated that this emerging land is everywhere higher than the whole level of the sea. Thirdly, an objection will be made to these demonstrations, and the objection will be answered, Fourthly, the final and efficient cause of this rising or emerging land will be shown. Fifthly, an answer will be given to the arguments mentioned above.

## Determination in Two Modes

§ x. I say then firstly that if the water, looked at as to its circumference, should be in any part higher than the land, this would be necessarily in one of these two modes: either that the water should be excentric, as the first and fifth reasons advanced; or that being concentric[12] it should be gibbous[13] in some part, in such a way that it should rise above the land; it could not be in any other way, as is abundantly clear to anyone who examines the matter deeply. But neither of these two modes is possible; therefore, neither is that from which, or by which, the other

# A Question of the Water and of the Land

followed. The consequence, as is said, is manifest through the argument[14] founded on a sufficient division of the cause; the impossibility of the consequent will appear through those things which will be shown.

## First and Second Supposition

§ xi, For the clearness of what is about to be said, two things are to be supposed. The first is that water is naturally moved downwards, the second is that water is of its nature a gliding body, and not brought to a stop of its own accord, And if anyone should deny these two bases, or either of them, the determination of the question will not be for him; because it cannot be disputed about any science with one who denies the very bases of that science, as is seen in the first book of the *Physics*;[15] because these bases are discovered by the senses and by the induction of those whose lot it is to discover such things, as is shown in the first book to Nichomacus.[16]

## Destruction of the First Member.

§ xii. To the destruction then, of the first member of the consequent, I say that it is impossible that the water can be excentric, which I demonstrate thus. If the water was excentric, three impossible things would follow, the first of which is that the water would naturally be movable upwards and downwards; the second is that the water would not be moved downwards by the same line with the land; the third is that weight would be ambiguously predicated of them; all which things are seen to be not only false, but impossible. The consequence is shown thus: Let the heavens be the circumference where the three crosses are placed, the water where there are two, the land where there is one, and let the center of the heavens and of the land be at the point A, but the centre of the water excentric[17] be at point B, as is shown in the accompanying figure. I say, then, that if there shall be water at A, and it has a passage, it will naturally be moved to B, because everything that is heavy is naturally moved to the centre of its own proper circum-

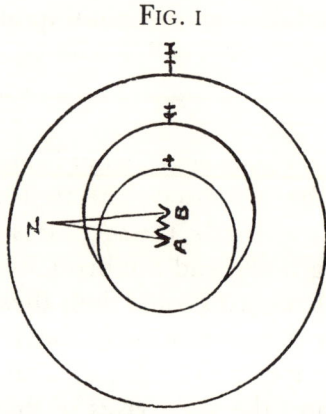

FIG. I

ference; and since the movement from A to B is a movement upwards, for A is simply the bottom of all things,[18] water will naturally be moved upwards, which was the first impossibility which was stated above. Next let there be a clod of earth at Z, and at the same place a quantity of water and no obstacle in the way. Since then, as was said, every heavy thing is moved towards the centre of its own proper circumference, the clod of earth will be moved by a straight line to A, and the water in a straight line to B. But this will happen by different lines, as is shown in the accompanying figure, which is not only impossible, but would make Aristotle laugh if he heard it; and this was the second matter which was to be made clear. The third matter, then, I show is this: heaviness and lightness are qualities of simple bodies, which are moved with a straight motion, and light things are moved up and heavy things down. For this I mean by heavy and light, namely, that which is movable, as the philosopher says in his *Cœlum et Mundum*.[19] So then the water would be moved to B, the clod of earth, on the other hand, to A; since both are heavy bodies, they will be moved downwards to different points, of which there cannot be one law, since one is downwards simply, the other in a manner peculiar to itself.[20] And since

# A Question of the Water and of the Land

diversity in the law of ends argues diversity in those things which are on account of them, it is manifest that there will be a different law of movement[21] in the water and in the land; and since diversity of law with identity of name makes an ambiguity, as is shown by the philosopher in his *Antepredicaments*,[22] it follows that weight is used ambiguously of the water and of the earth, which was the third member of the consequence to be declared. Thus, therefore, it appears by a true demonstration of their genus, by which I have shown that this is not, that is, that the water is not excentric, which was the first of the succeeding principal consequence which had to be destroyed.

## Destruction of the Second Member.[23]

§ xiii. To the destruction of the second member of the succeeding principal consequence I say that it is altogether impossible that the water is gibbous, which I thus

Fig. 2

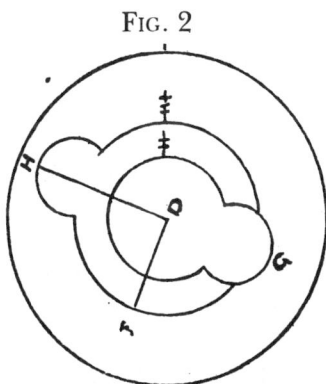

demonstrate.[24] Let the heavens be where there are four crosses, the water where there are three, and land where there are two, and the centre of the land and of the water concentric, and of the heavens, be at D. And let this be known beforehand that the water cannot be concentric with the land, unless the land be gibbous in some part above its central circumference, as is clear to those who are instructed in mathematics. If in any part the circumference of the water rises up, and so let the gibbousness of the water be at H, the gibbousness of the land at G; then let a line be drawn from D to H, and a line from D to F. It is manifest that the line which is from D to H is longer than that from D to F; and by this its summit is higher than the summit of the other; and since both of them touch in its summit the superficies of the water and do not pass beyond it, it is clear that the water is upwards with regard to the superficies where F is. When, therefore, there is nothing there to prevent it, if those things are true which were first assumed, the water of the gibbous part will flow down until it will be at a level at D,[25] with the central or regular circumference; and so it will be impossible for the gibbousness to remain or to be, which was to be demonstrated. And besides this most powerful demonstration, it can be shown probably[26] that the water has not a gibbousness outside its regular circumference; because that which can be done in one way it is better it *should* be done in one way than in several;[27] but all[28] might be done by the gibbousness only of the earth, as will appear below; therefore there is no gibbousness in the water, since God and Nature do and will that which is better,[29] as is shown by the philosopher in his *De Cœlo et Mundo*, and in his *De generatione Animalium*.[30] Thus, therefore, it is impossible for the water in any part of its circumference to be higher — that is, further from the centre of the world — than the surface of this habitable land is, which was the first in the order of the things to be said.

*He concludes that the Water is Concentric.*
§ xiv. If, therefore, it is impossible that the water is excentric, as was demonstrated by the first figure, or that it has any gibbousness, as by the second was demonstrated, it is necessary that it must be concentric and level — that is, equally distant from the centre of the world in every part of its circumference, as is clear of itself.
*He argues Contra; and first.*
§ xv. Now I argue in this way: whatever rises above

any part of a circumference which is equally distant from the centre, is more remote from that centre than any part of the circumference, But all the shores, both of Amphitrite herself,[31] as well as the shores of the mediterranean seas,[32] are above the level of the contiguous sea, as is patent to the eye: therefore all the shores are more remote from the centre of the world, since the centre of the world is also the centre of the sea (as has been seen), and the surface of the shores are parts of the whole surface of the sea. And since every thing which is more remote from the centre of the world is also higher, it follows that all the shores are above the whole sea, and if the shores, much more the other regions of the land; for the shores are the lower parts of the land, and this the rivers show, for they flow down to them. The major, indeed, of this demonstration is demonstrated by geometric theorems, and the demonstration is palpable to the senses, although it has its own force, as in those things which were demonstrated above *per impossibile*. And so it is clear of the second.

*He argues against the Things that have been Determined.*

§ xvi. But against these things that have been determined it is argued in this way: the heaviest body seeks the centre equally on all sides, and most powerfully. The land is the heaviest body; therefore it seeks the centre equally on all sides, and most powerfully. And from this conclusion it follows, as I shall make clear, that the land is equally distant from the centre in every part of its circumference, by that which is called *æqualiter*; and that it is the *substans*[33] of all bodies, by reason of that which is called *potissime*; from which it would follow (if the water was concentric as it is said to be) that the land would be covered and lying hid; the contrary of which we see. That these things follow from the conclusion I thus make clear. Let us postulate as the contrary, or opposite, of this conclusion, which is that it is equally distant in every part, and let us say that it is not distant; and let us postulate that at one part the surface of the land is distant twenty stadia,³⁴ and at another ten; and so that one hemisphere of it will be of greater quantity than the other, and it does not matter whether they differ little or much in distance so long as they do differ. Since, then, of the greater quantity of land there is a greater power of weight, the larger hemisphere, through the prevailing force of its weight, will press upon the smaller hemisphere, until the quantity of both shall become equal, by which equality the weight will become equal; and so on all sides it will be brought back to the distance of fifteen stadia, as we see in the weighing and adjusting of the weights in the balances. By which it is evident that it is impossible that land equally tending to the centre can be distant from it differently or unequally in its circumference. Therefore it is necessary that its opposite is unequally distant; which is to be equally distant when it may be distant;³⁵ and so the consequence is made clear from the part of that which is to be equally distant. Which also follows, that it is the *substans* of all bodies (which was also said to follow from the conclusion), so I declare. The most powerful virtue most powerfully attains its end; for through this it is most powerful, because it is the quickest, because most quickly and easily it can arrive at its end. The most powerful virtue of gravity is in a body which most powerfully tends to the centre, which indeed is the land; therefore it most powerfully attains the end of gravity which is the centre of the world; therefore it will be the *substans* of all bodies, if it most powerfully seeks the centre, which was to be made clear in the second place. So, therefore, it appears to be impossible that the water is concentric with the land, which is contrary to the things which have been determined.

*The preceding Reason is met by an Objection*³⁶

§ xvii. But this reason does not appear to demonstrate, because the proposition of the principal major in like manner does not seem to be necessary. For it was said that the heaviest body equally, everywhere, and most pow-

# A Question of the Water and of the Land 19

erfully tends to the centre, which does not seem to be necessary, because allowing that the land is the heaviest body compared with other bodies, yet compared with itself, that is with its different parts, it may be heaviest and not heaviest, because the land may be heavier in one part than in another. For, since the adequation of a heavy body is not made by quantity, *quâ* quantity, but by weight, there may be here an adequation of weight, where there may not be an adequation of quantity, and so this demonstration is apparent and not real.

## The Objection is Answered.

§ xviii. But such an objection is naught, for it proceeds from ignorance of the nature of homogeneous and simple bodies; for bodies are homogeneous and simple; homogeneous as purified gold, and simple bodies as fire and earth, which in their parts are regularly qualified by every natural quality. Whence, since the land is a body simple regularly in its parts, it is qualified naturally, and of itself, so to speak: wherefore, since gravity is inherent naturally in the land and the land is a simple body, it is necessary that it should have regular gravity in all its parts, according to the proportion of the quantity, and so the reason of the principal objection disappears. Whence it must be answered that the reason of the objection is sophistic, because it is fallacious, *secundum quid* and *simpliciter propter quod*.[37] It must be understood that universal Nature is not frustrated of its end; although particular Nature sometimes through the disobedience of matter is frustrated of its intended end, yet universal Nature in no way can fail of its intention, since both the act and potentiality of things,[38] which can and can not be, are subject to universal Nature. But the intention of universal Nature is that all forms which are in the potentiality of the first matter may be reduced into act, and may be in act according to the law of the species; that the first matter according to its whole totality may exist under every material form, although according to its part it may be under every opposite privation except one. For since all forms which in idea are in the potentiality of matter, are in act in the Mover of the Heavens, as says the commentator in his *De substantia orbis*;[39] if all these forms were not always in act, the Mover of the Heavens would fail in the completeness of the diffusion of His goodness,[40] which is not to be spoken of. And since all material forms of things which are generated and liable to corruption, except the forms of the elements, require matter and a mixed and complex subject, to which, as to its end, the elements are ordained, *quâ* elements; and a mixing cannot be where things are not capable of being mixed together, as is obvious of itself: it is necessary that in the universe there must be a part in which all things capable of being mixed, to wit, the elements, can come together; but this could not be unless the land in some part should emerge, as is evident to anyone who gives attention. Whence, since all Nature[41] obeys the intention of universal Nature it was necessary that besides the simple nature of the land which is to be downwards from above, there should be in it another nature by which it should be obedient to the intention of universal Nature; as, to wit, that it should be subject to be raised up in some part by the influence of the heavens, as if obedient to a teacher: as we see in the case of concupiscence and irascibility in man, which, though, through their own impetus they are carried away according to the sensitive affection, yet in so far as they are obedient to reason, they are sometimes drawn back from their own natural inclination[42] as appears in the first of the *Ethics*.[43]

§ xix. And so though the earth according to its simple nature tends equally to the centre, as was said in the argument of the objection, yet according to a certain nature it is subject to be raised up in part, obeying universal Nature, so that a mixing may be possible, and in this way the concentricity of the land and the water is preserved;

Fig. 3

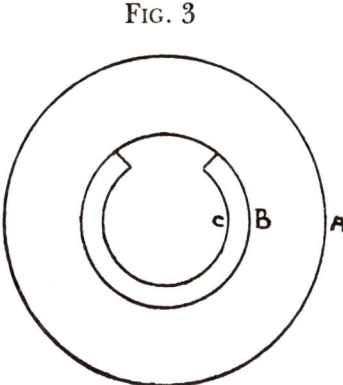

and nothing impossible follows with those who philosophise aright,[44] as is shown in this figure. Let the heavens be the circle where A is, the water the circle where is B, the land the circle where is C; and it matters not, as far as the true proposition is concerned, that the water should be little or far distant from the land. And let it be understood that this is true,[45] because it is such as is the form and site of the two elements, the two others above are false,[46] and are given not because it is so but that the learner may understand, as he says in the first book of the *Priores*.[47] And that the land emerges gibbously and not by a central circle of circumference is indubitably evident, when the figure of the emerging earth is considered. For the figure of the emerging earth is that of a half-moon, which it in no way could be, if it should emerge according to a regular or central circumference; for, as it is demonstrated in mathematical theorems, it is necessary that the regular circumference of a sphere should always emerge with a circular horizon from a plain or spheric superficies, such as the superficies of the water must be. And that the emerging earth should have a figure equal to that of a half-moon is manifest both from the naturalists who treat of it, and from astronomers who describe climates, and by geographers who mark the regions of the earth through all the different quarters. For as it is commonly held by all, this habitable world is extended by a longitudinal line from Gades which is placed above the western confines from Hercules,[48] up to the mouth of the river Ganges, as Orosius writes.[49] Which longitude indeed is so great that, while the sun is setting, when it is in the equinoctial line, to those who are at one of the termini, it is rising to those who are at the other, as was discovered by astronomers by the eclipse of the moon. Therefore it must be that the boundaries of the aforesaid longitude are distant 180 degrees, which is the half of the distance of the whole circumference. By the line indeed of latitude as we commonly have it from these same people[50] it extends[51] from those whose zenith is the equinoctial circle up to those whose zenith is a circle described from the pole of the Zodiac round the pole of the world,[52] which is distant from the pole of the world about 23 degrees, and so the extension of the latitude is about 67 degrees, and not more, as is clear to whoever pays attention. And so it is clear that the emerging land must have the figure of a half-moon, or thereabouts; because that figure is the result of so much latitude and longitude, as is evident. If, indeed, it should have a circular horizon, it would have a circular convex figure; and so the longitude and latitude would not differ in the distance of their boundaries, as it must be manifest even to women. And so it is clear concerning the third proposition in the order of things to be spoken of.

*Of the Efficient Cause of the Elevation of the Land.*
§ xx. It remains now to see about the final and efficient cause of this elevation of the land, which has been sufficiently demonstrated: and this is the artificial order; for the question whether it be, ought to precede the question why it is. And about the final cause, let those things suffice which have been said in the foregoing distinction.[53] For, indeed, to investigate the efficient cause, it must be noted first, that the present treatise is not outside natural matter, because it deals with mobile entities,[54] that is to say, the water and the land which are natural bodies, and about

# A Question of the Water and of the Land

these things certainty must be sought according to natural matter, which is here the subject matter; for in each kind of genus certainty must be sought only as far as the nature of the thing admits, as is clear from the first of the *Ethics*.[55] Since, then, innate in us is the course of investigating truth about natural things from those which are better known to us, but less known to Nature, to those which are more certain and better known to Nature, as is clear from the first of the *Physics*[56] and since in such things the effects are better known to us than the causes, because by them we are led to the knowledge of the causes, as is clear, for instance, the eclipse of the sun led to the knowledge of the interposition of the moon, whence from wondering men began to philosophize; the cause of investigation in natural matter ought to be from effects to causes. Which course, indeed, though it may have sufficient certainty yet hath it not so much as the course of inquiry in mathematics hath, which is from causes, or higher matters, to effects or lower things: and so that amount of certainty must be sought which can be obtained in such demonstration. I say then that the efficient cause of this elevation cannot be the land itself; because since the being elevated is a certain being carried upward, and to be carried upward is contrary to the nature of the land: and nothing speaking of it *per se*,[57] can be the cause of this, which is contrary to its own nature; it remains that the land cannot be the efficient cause of this elevation. And in like manner, too, neither can the water; because since water is a homogeneous body, it behoves that virtue should be uniformly in every part of it; speaking of it *per se*; and thus there would be no reason why it should elevate here more than elsewhere. This same reason removes both air and fire from this causality; and since there remaineth none other[58] but the heavens this effect must be reduced to them, as though to its own proper cause. But since there are many heavens it yet remaineth to inquire to which, as though to its own proper cause, it is to be reduced. Not to the heaven of the moon; because the moon herself is the organ of her own virtue or influence; and she declines as much through the Zodiac from the equinoctial towards the Antarctic pole, as towards the Arctic, so she would elevate[59] that side of the equinoctial as well as on this, which is not the fact. Nor does it avail to say that this declination cannot be because of its being nigher to the land through excentricity; for if there was this power of elevating in the moon (since nearer agents act more powerfully) it would elevate rather there than here.

§ xxi. This same reasoning removes from this kind of causality all the orbs of the planets; and since the *Primum Mobile*, that is the ninth sphere, is uniform throughout, and consequently uniformly imbued with power throughout, there is no reason why it should draw up more on one part than another. Since then there are no other mobile bodies except the heaven of the fixed stars, which is the eighth sphere, this effect must of necessity be reduced to that. For the evidence of which thing it should be known that while the heaven of the fixed stars hath unity in substance it hath also multiplicity in power, on which account it behoved that it should have that diversity in its parts which we see, so that through divers organs divers powers it might shed abroad: and he who does not recognize these things, let him know he is outside the limits of philosophy. In it we see difference in the magnitude and in the light of stars, in the figures and images of constellations; which differences indeed cannot be for naught, as must be manifest to all who have been nurtured in philosophy. Whence different is the power of this star from the power of that, of this constellation and of that; and different is the power of the stars which are on this side of the equinoctial line, from those which are on that. Wherefore since the aspects of the inferior are similar to the aspects of the superior, as Ptolemæus says, it follows that this effect cannot be traced back to anything save to the heaven of the stars, as we have seen; because the similitude of the virtual agent dwells in that region of the heavens which operates upon this uncovered land. And since this uncovered land is extended from the equinoctial line to the line which the pole of the Zodiac describes round the pole of the world, as was said above; it is manifest that there is an elevating power in these stars, which are in the region of the heavens contained by these two circles, whether it draweth up by way of attraction, as the magnet draws the iron, or by way of compulsion, by generating compelling vapours, as in some mountain parts.[60] But now it is asked: if that region of the heavens is moved in a circle why was not the elevation circular? I answer it was not circular because the material did not suffice for so great an elevation. But then it is further argued, and the question put: why was the hemispheral elevation rather on this side than on another? To this it is to be said, as the philosopher says in his second book of the heavens,[61] when one asks why the heavens are moved from the east to west and not the other way: where he says, indeed, that such like questions proceed either from much foolishness or great presumption, because they are above our intellect. So to this question it must be said, that as God the glorious disposer, who determined the place of the nations, the position of the centre of the world, the distance of the extreme circumference of the universe from its centre, and other such like things, did them for the best, so also did He these. Thus when He said, "Let the waters be gathered together in one place, and let the dry land appear," so the heavens were endowed with virtue for to do, and the land with power to be patient.

§ xxii. Let them cease then, let men cease to inquire into those matters which are above them, and let them seek so far as is within their grasp, that where'er they can they may draw[62] themselves up to things immortal and divine, and leave those which are too great for them. Let them hearken to friend Job where he says, "Wouldst thou comprehend the footsteps of God, and find out the Omnipotent even to perfection?" Let them hearken to the Psalmist saying, "Thy wisdom is made wonderful, and has been my comfort, and I shall not be able to attain to it." Let them hear Isaiah saying, "As far as the heavens are distant from the earth so far are my ways from Thy ways." It was spoken indeed in the person of God to men. Let them hear the voice of the Apostle to the Romans, "Oh height of the riches of the knowledge and wisdom of God, how incomprehensible His judgments and His ways not to be sought out!" And lastly let them hear the voice of the Creator saying, "Whither I go ye cannot come." And let these things suffice in the search of the truth ye strain after.

§ xxiii. These things being seen it is easy to refute the above made arguments on the other side, which was proposed to be done in the fourth place. When, therefore, it was said that there cannot be the same centre to two circumferences unequally distant from one another, I say that is true if the circumferences are regular without hump or humps. And when it is said in the minor that the circumference of the water, and the circumference of the land, are of this kind, I say this is not true, unless through a gibbousness which is in the land, and so the argument does not proceed. To the second, when it is said: To the nobler body a nobler place is due, I say it is true according to its own proper nature, and I concede the minor; but when the conclusion is drawn that therefore the water ought to be in a higher place, I say that it is true according to the proper nature of either body; but by a supereminent cause (as was said above) it comes to pass that in this part[63] the land is higher; and so the argument was defective in the first proposition. To the third when it is said: Every opinion which is contradictory to the sense is a bad opinion, I say this argument proceeds from a false imagination. For sailors imagine when they are at sea that they do not see the land from the ship because the sea is higher than the land, but this is not so; indeed it would be the contrary, for they would rather see it. But this is because the direct ray of the visible object is broken between the object and the eye from the convexity of the water; for since it behoves that

# A Question of the Water and of the Land

the water must have a round form everywhere about the centre, it is necessary that at a certain distance it should create an obstacle by its convexity. To the fourth when it was argued: If the land was not lower &c; I say that this argument is founded in falsity; and so is naught. For the common people and the ignorant of physical arguments believe that water may ascend to the tops of mountains, and even to the place of fountains in the form of water; but this is very childish, for the waters are generated there (as is shown by the philosopher in his Meteors[64]), the matter ascending in the form of vapour. To the fifth where it is said that the water is a body which follows the orb of the moon; and from that it is concluded that it must be excentric; I say this reason has no necessity, because although a thing may imitate another in one particular it is not on that account necessary that it should imitate it in everything. We see that fire imitates the circular motion of the heavens, and yet it does not imitate them in not moving in a straight line, nor in not having the contrary of its own quality,[65] and so the reason proceeds not. And so much for the arguments. Thus therefore is determined the determination and the treatise on the form and site of the two elements, as was proposed above.

§ xxiv. This philosophy was determined when the unconquered Lord Duke Cane Grandi de Scala was ruling for the most holy Roman Emperor by me Dante Alagherius, least of philosophers, in the renowned city of Verona, in the Church of the Glorious Helena, before the whole Veronese clergy, except certain ones who burning with a too great charity,[66] admit not the questions of others, and poor by virtue of the humility of the Holy Spirit, lest they should seem to approve the excellence of others, refuse to mix themselves up in their discourses. And this was made in the year from the nativity of our Lord Jesus Christ the thousandth three hundredth and twentieth, on Sunday, which our aforesaid Savior through His glorious nativity, and by His wondrous resurrection hath intimated to us as by a sign that we should venerate it; which day was the seventh from the ides of January and the thirteenth before the kalends of February.

## NOTES
1. This heading is, of course, an addition of an editor. The first edition, that by Manfred de Monteferrato in 1508, is headed — *Quæstio florulenta ac perutilis de duobus elementis acquæ et terræ tractans*, &c.
2. Aristotle's *Categoriæ*. Dante refers again to the *doctrina prædicamentorum* in his *De Monarchi*a, III. xv. 55.
3. See Introduction.
4. *I.e.* the centre of the earth.
5. Aristotle, *De Cœlo*, II. xiii, 3.
6. *Cœlum primum*, the heaven of the moon (see Introduction).
7. *Quasi manifeste*. Longhena translates this *quasi manifestamente si excludevano*. This cannot be Dante's meaning. At § xxiii when he deals with this second reason he conditionally admits the truth of the major premise, "to the more noble body a more noble place is fitting," and concedes the minor, "The water is a more noble body than the land." *Manifeste* stands for *manifestæ*.
8. Aristotle's treatise *De Anima*, the commentator is Averroes (see note 42).
9. Aristotle's *Meteorologica*, where he says: καὶ διότι τελεμτ ή μάλλον μdατος ή ὖqvp έqτim ή θάκαττα.
10. Than that of which it is the principle or origin.
11. *I.e.* having its circumference not at all parts equally distant from its center.
12. All the texts appear to read *excentrica existens*. I venture to conjecture that this is an error for *concentrica*. The diagram and the argument in § xiii., *quod aqua non potest esse concentrica terræ, nisi sit in aliqua parte gibbosa* . . . confirm the reading I suggest.
13. *I.e.* with a hunch or part protruding beyond the regular line of its circumference.
14. *Per Locum* — for the various logical uses of *Locum* see *The Topics* of Cicero, 2 *et seq.*
15. Aristotle's *Physics*, I, ii.

# A Question of the Water and of the Land

16. Aristotle's *Nichomachean Ethics*, I, vii. 21.

17. *I.e.* having a center different from the common center of the universe and the land.

18. Because it is the centre of the universe.

19. There is no such work by Aristotle to whom Dante always applies this title, the quotation is from his work *De Cœlo*, IV. i., The book *De Mundo*, which has often passed as a work of Aristotle, was much later (see Introduction).

20. *Secundum quid.*

21. *Ratio fluitatis.*

22. Aristotle's *Categoricæ*, I. 1-4.

23. That the water is gibbous.

24. Dr. Moore says (*Studies in Dante*, p. 128), "The diagram and argument based upon it is taken almost directly from the *De Cœlo*, II. iv. (287 b, 4-14)"; but here this generally accurate writer is strangely in error. Aristotle is seeking to prove another point in the chapter cited; the diagram he describes is totally different, while the argument which it illustrates there is only a very slight connection with the following argument of Dante. Indeed, the sentence quoted in the following note is nearly the only common ground between the two passages.

25. ὥϛτε peqiqqeύreται τϛ ὑάxq ἐxy εν irarhή. *De Cœlo*, II. iv. 12.

26. *Probabiliter*, with probability as opposed to certainty.

27. See *De Mon*. I. xvi. (at the beginning), *Et quod potest fieri per unum, melius est fieri per unum quam per plura*. Both these quotations are from Aristotle's *De partibus Animalium*, III. iv. 5.

28. *Totum oppositum potest fieri.*

29. Aristotle, *De Cœlo*, I. i. 6.

30. Aristotle, *De generatione Animalium*, II. vi. 38.

31. Amphitrite, the goddess of the sea, put for the ocean itself.

32. *Marium mediterraneorum*, inland seas generally.

33. *Substans*, standing under, supporting *æqualiter*, equally; *potissime*, most strongly.

34. The stadium — *i.e.* the Olympic stadium — was 606¾ feet.

35. *Quod est æqualiter distare, quum distet.* The whole of this paragraph is probably corrupt, or possibly added to by a later hand.

36. *Per instantiam*, an objection. Aristotle, *Anal. pr.* II. xxvi.

37. *I.e.* it confuses the incidents of homogeneous and simple bodies; it argues from a proposition which applies only in certain particular cases as though it applied in all cases, and thus is fallacious *secundum quid*; and it assigns a wrong reason for the phenomena it seeks to explain, and so is fallacious *simpliciter propter quod*.

38. *Actus et potentia*. *Potentia*, the possibility of becoming to be of a certain kind or in a certain way, or power of doing an act, whether in use or not; *actus*, the being or the act itself; the putting the *potentia* into force.

39. The *De substantia orbia* of Averroes. *Averrois che l'gran commento feo, Inf.* iv. The "form" in logic is that which makes a thing to be what it is. Thus a statue is in potentiality in the marble before it becomes by act a statue; when it receives its form, it becomes that which it is — a statue.

40. *Deficeret ab integritate diffusionis suæ bonitatis*, that is, if the Creator allowed His power to remain in abeyance, in potentiality, and not in act, His goodness would not be fully diffused.

41. All the particular or individual parts of Nature. The distinction between universal and particular Nature is taken from the *Physics* of Albertus Magnus, Lib. ii. Tract. i., cap. v. See Dr. Moore's *Studies in Dante*. The same distinction is made in *Conv.* I. vii. In *Conv.* III. iv. he says *la natura universale cioè Iddio*. Compare also *Conv.* IV. ix and IV. xxvi *ordinato per provvedimento di natura universale che ordina la particulare alla sua perfezione*. And see note to this last passage in Fraticelli's edition.

42. *A proprio impetus*. Longhena translates this: *talvolta per impeto proprio*, which spoils the argument.

43. Aristotle's *Ethics,* I. xiii. 15-17. And see *Ethics,* VII. 1-6 *seq*.

44. No impossible result ensues when one considers these things philosophically.

45. *I.e.* the figure.

46. The two other figures.

47. Aristotle's *Prior Analytics.*

48. The Pillars of Hercules.

49. Orosius, *Adversus Paganos*, I. ii. 7-13. *Europæ in Hispania occidentalis oceanus termino est, maxime ubi apud Gades insulas*

# A Question of the Water and of the Land

*Herculis columnæ visuntur . . . Asia ad mediam frontem orientis habet in oceano Eoo ostia fiumina Gangis.*

50. Astronomers.

51. The earth.

52. The pole of the Zodiac, or the pole of the ecliptic as it is generally called, is an imaginary pole at a point where a perpendicular line drawn from the sign of Pisces cuts the Arctic circle. A glance at the celestial globe will show the bearing of this argument better than a long note would. It will there be seen how the land part of the world appeared to be in Dante's time, something like the part marked C in Fig. 3.

53. *Præmediata distinctione.* The Oxford edition reads *præmeditata.*

54. *Inter ens mobile,* i.e., material being.

55. Aristotle's *Ethics,* I. iii. 4. And compare *Con.* IV. xiii.ll. 49-50. *Il disciplinato chiede di sapere certezza nelle cose secondochè la loro natura di certezza receva.* And *De Mon.* II. ii. ll. 40-41. *Non similiter in omni materia certitude quærenda est, sed secundum quod natura rei subjectæ recipit.*

56. Aristotle's *Physics,* I. i. Fraticelli's reading of this passage, and Longhena's translation of it, are both hopeless. Dr. Moore improves the text by putting a comma after *notis* and *ad*, which had doubtless dropped out by mistake, before *certiora*, and which corresponds with the ἐπι in the *Physics*; but by placing a full stop at *philosophari* he leaves the sentence incomplete and without its governing verb. By putting a comma after *phil-osophari*, and no full stop till *potest*, we get as the statement of the whole sentence, *viam inquisitionis oportet esse*, and though it is monstrously long it makes sense. The meaning I take to be that since principles are better known to Nature than details, while it is the reverse to us, we must reason from effects to causes, and not, as Nature is assumed to do, from causes to effects. The following is the passage in Aristotle:

> Πέυτκε δέ τών cνωϙιμωτέϙων ἡμῖν ἡ ὁδόγ καὶ rauertέϙων ἐρίτά rauérteϙa τῇ ύϐrei κάι cνωϙιμώτεϙa . . . : ἀνάcκϙ τόν τρόον τόττον pϙcάceiv ἐκ των ἀrauertέϙων μέν τῇ ύϐrei ἡμῖν δέ rauértεϙων ἐρί τά rauértea . . . κ. τ. k.

57. I have adopted the punctuation of the Oxford text.

58. *Et quum non restet alterius nisi cœlum,* Dr. Moore suggests reading *ulterius,* though what sense he would make of it does not

appear *Cœlum* likewise he takes to mean the fifth element, or the άίθήρ, but this is inconsistent with the context.

59. *I.e.* would raise the land up as much on the south of the equator, as on the north, which Dante assumes *non est factum*.

60. Aristotle's *Meteorica*, II. viii, *conf. Purg.* xxi. 56, *per vento che in terra si nasconda*.

61. Aristotle's *De Cælo*, II. v. Rather a free translation.

62. *Ut trahant se ad immortalia et divina pro posse. Conf. Convito* IV. xiii. *e pero dice Aristotle nel decimo dell'*Etica, *contra Simonide poeta parlando, che l'uomo si dee traere alle divine cose quanto puo*. Taken from Aristotle's *Ethics*, X. vii. 8, or rather from Aristotle through St. Thomas Aquinas in his *Summa contra gentiles*. *Philosophus dicit quod homo debet se ad* immortalia *et* divina *trahere* quantum potest. See Dr. Moore's *Studies in Dante* on the evidence of this, and other passages, to the genuineness of the *Questio*.

63. The inhabitable part of the earth.

64. Aristotle's *Meteorologica*, I. ix.

65. Fire sometimes has a circular motion, sometimes it moves in a straight line, and while its nature is upwards and in a pyramidical form, yet often it moves in another direction.

66. Longhena translates this *di troppo amore di se*, which is incorrect and spoils the intense sarcasm of the original.

PART TWO

*DANTE'S INFLUENCE
ON AMERICAN WRITERS
1776 - 1976*

(EDITED AND WITH AN INTRODUCTION BY ANNE PAOLUCCI)

## Introduction

### ANNE PAOLUCCI
(Vice President, Dante Society of America)

My impression has long been that the *Divine Comedy* tempts all of us who read it appreciatively in any language — for its greatness survives translation — to take the trip subjectively: to re-imagine our past lives, and to project our futures, in Dantesque terms. If we didn't know we were lost in a dark wood and had to take *un altro viaggio,* another course, down through Hell and back up to our present purgatory, Dante shows us that it is indeed so, like it or not. If we haven't found ourselves gone astray, in Dante's irresistible grasp of our mind's eye, we find ourselves finding ourselves — *ci ritroviamo – in una selva oscura,* in a dark wood.

Dante's odyssey, much more than Odysseus,' is our odyssey. I was reminded of this just a few days ago, reading something of the resurrected old dispute about Alger Hiss, Whittaker Chambers, and the Pumpkin papers. Chambers, you may recall, high up in the *Time*-magazine world, at one point decided to tell his tale in a book called *Witness,* which was to be the truth, the whole truth and nothing but the truth about his underground life to that time. And to do it, I had noted on first reading, he had felt constrained to pour the whole business directly into the artistic mould of Dante's *Inferno.*

In his opening paragraph, Chambers speaks of experiencing the "fears, uncertainties, self-doubts, cowardices, flinchings of the will — natural to any man who undertakes to reverse in mid-course the journey of his life," at the same time that he feels "a surging release and a sense of freedom, like the man who bursts, at last gasp, out of a drowning sea." Chambers doesn't cite the Dantesque source for those two images; but that doesn't make his *Witness* any less artful.

Late in the book, Chambers tells of his long sessions with the FBI, the reports of which made a fair-sized book. When he had re-read the transcript, he was asked whether he wished to add anything. Chambers took the interrogator's pen, he tells us, and at the end of the report wrote in Italian: "*E quindi uscimmo a riveder le stelle.*" ("And so we came forth again to see the stars.") Chambers then says (in a footnote):

> This literary flourish may seem more understandable when the context of that experience is remembered, and when it is recalled that these words are the last line of Dante's *Inferno* and the last line of Marx's *Capital*.

That note is perhaps the most revealing moment in the 800 pages of *Witness*, which concludes a few pages later with a passage that reads: "I have been seeing a good deal of the stars of late . . . both the evening and the morning stars."

With that, I turn to our three presentations which sample more aptly I think the range of the Dantesque influence on American writers. With Professor Cambon's paper we will get a sense of Dante's direct influence on the writing and politics of a contemporary poet — Galway Kinnell — where the parallels are very close. But before that, we will learn about the all-pervasive influence of Dante on Ezra Pound and T. S. Eliot, who are ours, even though they have sought the laurel elsewhere. And before that, too, we shall learn something of Dante's influence on writers of an earlier time in this once brave new world of ours which — in this bicentenary year — has contributed admirably to what has been the latest and perhaps greatest continuing Dante revival in a long series.

## Opening Remarks

### Dr. Alessandro Cortese de Bosis,
(Consul General of Italy in New York)

Ladies and Gentlemen;

Let me say how grateful I am to the Dante Society and in particular to Anne Paolucci, who incidentally bears a proud Dantesque name, for their kind invitation. It is very fitting and not without elegance that the year of the Bicentennial should come to an end with a celebration in New York of a poet who wrote about life, liberty and the eternal pursuit of happiness, 400 years before the great Virginian. New York, the Universal City, thus honors, thanks to your society, Alighieri, the Universal Man, one of those very few to whom so much is owed by so many everywhere.

From Paradise where Dante has probably been assigned his lodgings, our poet will certainly follow with interest your proceedings. The very name of your town would be familiar to him: one of the characters he refers to so often in the *Divine Comedy*, the first Christian Emperor Constantine, was proclaimed Emperor in a city which is the namesake of New York.

But I know that your learned society, while cultivating the image of a poet who has inspired so many of your major writers from Longfellow to Lowell, to Norton to Pound, has no intention to confine itself to the cult of Dante. The *Divine Comedy* is certainly one of the summits reached by human creativity, but on its wake other great contributions, modern and contemporary, made by Italian writers should be explored by American scholars and readers. Dr. Paolucci, (also President of The Pirandello Society), who has done so much to diffuse the work of

American authors in Italy, should boldly put the question, "Who is Afraid of Dante Alighieri?" and encourage more and more the critical reading of other writers in Dante's language like Buzzati, Pratolini, Montale, Pavese to name just a few, who I'm afraid are not so well known as they deserve in this country. Needless to say, in this work of furthering the appreciation and knowledge of our literature, the Dante Society can count on the enthusiastic contribution of our Embassy in Washington and the Consulate General and the Institute of Culture in New York, represented here by its new dynamic Director, Professor Marco Miele, who incidentally comes from Florence and therefore digs Dante's Tuscan like a native.

On this note of confidence and on this promise of a stronger and stronger cultural solidarity between our Institutions, let me conclude by wishing the Dante Society of America, its officers and their families, a very happy New Year, full of further successes for their worthy enterprise.

## Greetings

### THE HON. LESTER WOLFF
(House of Representatives, 6th District, New York)

On December 28, 1976, I had the honor and privilege of participating in the special bicentennial program of The Dante Society of America.

Such names as St. Thomas Aquinas, Michelangelo, Da Vinci, Raphael, Galileo, and, supremely, Dante represent the heights which humankind has attained. Dante especially occupies a unique place in the history of Western culture and of Italy. To his then disunited homeland he gave a profound national consciousness as well as its greatest national poem. It has been well said that he found Italian a dialect and made it a language. However, his appeal is more than local: it is universal. Ranked with the greatest poets of antiquity, he stands as the first classical poet of the modern age. In the *Divine Comedy* he wrote perhaps the greatest epic, the vitality of which endures as we today approach the 21st century.

In this Bicentennial era, all Americans, whatever their ethnic or national origins, are increasingly aware of the contributions which each group has made to the common heritage. Italians have entered into every area of national life with distinction, often in the face of prejudice and discrimination. Nearly five million have come to these shores from Italy, seeking a new life and bringing traditions, customs, and ideals which have become part of America. Zest for life, deep love and loyalty for family, a willingness to work — these are among the qualities by which Italians have enriched this Nation.

Mark Twain once said "The Creator made Italy from designs by Michael Angelo." Certainly it is true that the spirit of Italy reflects the essential character of her people, whose contributions to human civilization are rightly honored throughout the world. The role of Italy and of the Italians in the history of mankind is a glorious one.

"You dreamed dreams," said President Wilson (addressing a group of new citizens), "of what America was to be, and I hope you brought the dreams with you. No man that does not see visions will ever realize any high hope or undertake any high enterprise. Just because you brought dreams with you, America is more likely to realize dreams such as you brought. You are enriching us if you came expecting us to be better than we are." Like Dante himself, Italian Americans have brought together past and present, looking in hope toward the future.

## Greetings

### THE HON. MARIO BIAGGI
(House of Representatives, 10th District, New York)

It is a great honor for me to be associated with the outstanding work of The Dante Society of America and in particular with this bicentennial tribute to the importance of Dante's poetic legacy for American writers. Dr. Anne Paolucci is to be commended for her work with the Society and for insuring the publication of this important event. The volume will provide each of us who had the pleasure to participate in the Bicentennial meeting on December 28, 1976 with a lasting record of that memorable event.

Dante's influence on modern poetry is indeed profound. The founders of The Dante Society of America — poets, scholars, and philosophers of great renown in their own right — saw the need to promote renewed interest and their labors have borne rich fruit. By enlightening us on the history of Dante, the Society has greatly increased our understanding of the roots of this nation's freedom. It was Dante who so eloquently wrote about life, liberty and the pursuit of happiness — the fundamental principles embodied in our Declaration of Independence.

Much has changed since Dante's lifetime. The world has seen many translations in the art of poetry. But throughout the centuries, the work of Dante has not only endured; it has served to inspire many a poet.

The Dante Society and its illustrious Vice President, Dr Anne Paolucci, are worthy of the highest praise for their endeavors. I wish the members and friends of the Society continued success in the years ahead.

A Historical Overview of
American Writers Interest in Dante
(to About 1900)

J. CHESLEY MATHEWS

We should like on this occasion review the beginning of the interest in Dante's writings shown by people in the United States, particularly by the major men of letters, and to trace the growth of this interest through most of the nineteenth century, to a time when a Dante tradition had become firmly established here.

The awakening m the United States of interest in Dante followed close upon a revival of interest in Dante in Europe. During the seventeenth century, when our country was being colonized, Dante's fame in Europe seems to have been at its lowest point. It was in the latter part of the eighteenth century that his reputation began to rise again — in Italy, France, Germany, and England; and in the nineteenth century, in all of these countries, the interest in Dante grew rapidly and greatly. Considering these facts, we should not expect any attention to be paid to Dante in the United States before the end of the eighteenth century. And the fact is that it *was* very late in the eighteenth century that the United States began to discover Dante.

One indication of the awakening of American interest in Dante was the acquisition of printed copies of some of his works. So far I have located only three items in the United States before 1800: the Library Company of Philadelphia had Boyd's translation of the *Inferno* in 1789 and a copy of the *Divina Commedia* in Italian in 1795, and Governor Edward Rutledge of South Carolina had a set of Dante's *Opere* before 1800. After 1800 we in America acquired more and more Dante books; and to see how our interest in Dante grew, one needs only to look at the catalogues of the Harvard Dante Collection and the Fiske Collection at Cornell — not to mention the collections in other Universities throughout the nation, in the Library of Congress, and in certain public libraries — for instance, the one in Boston.

Another indication of the beginning and growth of American interest in Dante was the publication of magazine articles about him, quotations and bits of translation from him, original verse inspired by him, and so forth. In all the seventeenth century, one item is known to have appeared: just a verse and a half from the *Paradiso*, quoted in Italian and in English in the *New York Almanac* for 1697. In all the eighteenth century, one item appeared: a verse translation of 34 lines of the Ugolino story, published in the *New York Magazine* in 1791. And as early as 1797, or a little earlier, the Ugolino story was translated into prose, although this translation was not published. (For the discovery of these three facts we are indebted to Professor Joseph Fucilla.) In the first decade of the nineteenth century, according to Koch's bibliography, *two* items were published; and in the following decades of the century, in order, *three* items, *seven, fourteen, twenty-seven, thirty-two, fifty-four, fifty-four, one hundred thirty-five*, and in just the first half of the tenth decade, *one hundred eight.*

It is of interest also to observe who were the early readers, students, and teachers of Dante in the United States. We do not know whether John Clapp and William Dunlap read more of Dante than the single passages they published in 1697 and 1791; but Richard Alsop presumably read more than the Ugolino passage, which he translated, for he translated other Italian works. As early as 1807 Benjamin Welles, of Boston, seems to have read Boyd's translation of the *Inferno* — possibly of the whole *Commedia* — and had read at least some of the *Inferno* in Italian. And Thomas Jefferson is said to have admired the *Divina Commedia* and read at least parts of it at some time before

1815.

The first person who is known to have taught Dante in our country was Lorenzo Da Ponte. During his approximately twenty-five years of teaching, beginning in 1807, he sought to inspire his pupils with enthusiasm for the *Divina Commedia* especially; and according to his testimony, they loved, admired, and studied it very much, and more than any other work of Italian literature.

George Ticknor was the second person who is believed to have taught Dante here and was our first Dante scholar. He had tried in vain to get help in reading that poet's work before he left Boston in 1815; but after reaching Europe he studied Italian, and Dante. Entering upon his duties as Professor of Modern Languages at Harvard, he is said to have "first introduced Dante to his students in 1819 in a general course on the great European poets"; and at least as early as the autumn term of 1831 to have delivered a whole course of lectures on the Italian master for a college class, and continued to do so in his three remaining years there. He remained an eager student of Dante for the rest of his life — for example, with a knowledge of all the principal commentaries on Dante, he prepared notes for the *Inferno* and *Purgatorio*; and he read Prince John of Saxony's translation of, and notes on, the *Commedia*. But when he resigned his professorship, he put a limit to his influence as a teacher, and he never published any results of his Dante studies.

After he left Harvard, the course in Dante was carried on by Henry Wadsworth Longfellow, beginning in 1838. Meanwhile, Pietro Bachi, instructor under Ticknor and Longfellow, from 1826 to 1846, was having the students in his course in Italian read the *Inferno*.

Another early student of Dante was W. H. Prescott, the historian, who read the *Divina Commedia* during the winter of 1823-24. The impression the poem made upon him at that time was never lost, wrote George Ticknor: "He never ceased to talk of Dante in the same tone of admiration in which he . . . broke forth on the first study of him." Then a few months later he regularly attended the readings of Italian poetry which were held three or four times a week in Ticknor's home, and at which large portions of the *Divina Commedia* were gone over. He was greatly impressed by the simple style of the poem, by the beauty of its "unrivalled similes," and its allusions to familiar objects; and he perceived that "to have read the *Inferno* is not to have read Dante"; that while the *Inferno* is more entertaining, and superior to the other two parts in narrative and action, the *Purgatorio* excels in giving "delicious descriptions of natural scenery" and "sober meditation," and the *Paradiso* in doing the impossible — picturing "purely intellectual delight." He also made some use of his knowledge of the *Commedia* in his writings, principally in his articles on "Italian Narrative Poetry" and "Poetry and Romance of the Italians." In the latter article, moreover, he once referred to the *Convito*, giving page references for a particular edition, and once to the *De Vulgari Eloquentia*, thus suggesting that he might have read those works.

Margaret Fuller was both a student and teacher of Dante. She first read the *Divina Commedia* probably in 1825 or soon afterward, and in 1836 she was, according to Emerson, "a dear student of Dante." One winter, while employed in Mr. Alcott's school in Boston, she formed a class in Italian, with which she read, among other things, "the whole hundred cantos" of the *Commedia*; and in her famous "conversations," held in Boston, she gave some attention to Dante. She also read the *Vita Nuova*, at least as early as 1842, and later wrote that it had been "one of the most cherished companions of [her] life." In 1845, moreover, she got copies of Cary's translation of the *Commedia* and Lyell's translation of Dante's "Lyrical poems," and wrote a short review of them for the *New York Tribune*.

Richard Henry Wilde, too, of Georgia, deserves to be remembered as a student of Dante and also as a minor poet whose work shows a little Dantean influence. He seems to have read at least some of the *Divina Commedia* before 1835, for the first stanza of his "Lines for the Music of Weber's Last Waltz" was modeled, he wrote, on the passage in Canto VIII of the *Purgatorio* "commencing *Era gia l'ora*." About the beginning of 1836 he began a five-year residence in Italy; and after spending some time upon a study of Tasso, he began "translating specimens of the Italian lyric poets, and composing short biographical notices of each author; and being much puzzled with the obscurities and contradictions abounding in the ordinary lives of Dante, it occurred to [him] to seek in the archives . . . whatever explanations they might afford." In carrying out this purpose, he came to desire to write a life of Dante, and then decided to include in the work a history of Dante's times.

The biographical sketch which he originally set out to write for the *Italian Lyric Poets* was never done — or else has been lost; but he did translate for the anthology two little poems by Dante, and a third poem then thought to be Dante's. *The Life and Times of Dante* was never finished either, but only about half done — unless the manuscript of some of it has been lost. But if Wilde never realized his ambition to complete and publish this work, just his laboring at the task led him to read Dante's writings, and many things written about them, their author, and his age. And Wilde's studies also led him to make an unexpected contribution of another kind. Through his reading he learned of the former existence of a portrait of Dante in the Bargello, and so he was led to initiate the undertaking which culminated in the discovery of the portrait by Giotto.

One should notice, moreover, that in Wilde's long original poem *Hesperia* there are five passages which contain echoes from the *Purgatory* and *Inferno*, and two other Dante references; that two quotations from the *Purgatory* and *Paradise* are quoted in his book on Tasso; that there are several references to, or quotations from, the *Divine Comedy*, the *De Vulgari Eloquentia*, and the *Convivio* in his biographical sketches in the *Italian Lyric Poets*; and that in the manuscript of his *Life and Times of Dante* there are nearly one hundred references to or quotations from six of Dante's works.

Still another important student of Dante was Thomas W. Parsons, of Boston, who was also a minor poet whose poems were considerably influenced by Dante. At the age of seventeen he went with his father on a year's visit to Europe, and spent the early months of 1837 in Italy. While there he became devoted to Dante, and started to memorize the *Commedia* and to translate it into English; and he continued to work at the translation after returning home. In 1843 he brought out *The First Ten Cantos of the Inferno*, which was the earliest published American translation of any considerable portion of Dante. Later he finished the first *canticle*, did nearly all of the *Purgatorio*, and a little of the *Paradiso*. He also turned into English verse at least two short passages from the *Vita Nuova*. And forty-one of his original poems show Dantean influence. One of them, "On a Bust of Dante," is well known. Its closing stanza, which refers to Dante's fame throughout the world, is a beautiful tribute:

> O Time! whose verdicts mock our own,
> The only righteous judge art thou;
> That poor old exile, sad and lone,
> Is Latium's other Virgil now:
> Before his name the nations bow;
> His words are parcel of mankind,
> Deep in whose hearts, as on his brow,
> The marks have sunk of Dante's mind.

Let us now consider the interest in Dante shown by our major men of letters of the period.

James Fenimore Cooper was the only one of the major figures who did not show an interest in the Italian poet.

Washington Irving read at least the *Inferno* in Italian in 1823 and 1825, owned a copy of the *Commedia*, and both revealed an interest in Dante and made some use of his knowledge of Dante — in one story, in one letter, in one magazine article, and in his book on Oliver Goldsmith. And he was impressed by the "horrible verity . . . of some of the tragic fictions of Dante," the severe grandeur, austere majesty, and touching beauties of Dante's poem.

William Cullen Bryant began studying Italian and reading Dante in 1825, and in 1826 he published a translation of six lines of *Purgatorio* VIII. Later he spoke of reading "the greater part of Dante" (that is, presumably, the *Commedia*); he knew at least one long passage from Dante by heart; in his anthology of poetry he included two quotations from *Inferno* III and V in Cary's translation; he read at least parts of Parsons' and Longfellow's translations; and in 1865 he wrote a little poem, "Dante," in which he praised the Italian poet as an apostle of liberty.

Ralph Waldo Emerson began reading Dante in 1818, and continued to be interested in Dante's work for the rest of his life. He acquired two Italian editions of the *Commedia*, an Italian edition of the *Vita Nuova*, and several volumes .of translations (by Cary, Parsons, Carlyle, and Norton). There are in Emerson's writings about 175 references to Dante, and nine quotations from the *Divine Comedy*. Emerson admired Dante's courage, force, symmetry, vivid perception, graphic description, recognition of the symbolic character of things, and his universality. He regarded "the new importance of the genius of Dante . . . to Americans" as one of the events of culture in the nineteenth century. There are a few passages in Emerson's writings which seem to echo specific lines of Dante. And most exciting of all, in 1843 Emerson translated the *Vita Nuova*, before any complete translation of the work into English had been published either in America or in Europe.

Nathaniel Hawthorne, in his writings, referred to Dante about a dozen times, beginning in 1835. He certainly knew the *Inferno*, and probably knew all of the

*Commedia.* He appreciated the ironic appropriateness of the punishments of hell, and at least some of Dante's symbolism — for example, the symbolic use of darkness, light, and colors. And at least three or four passages in Hawthorne's writings seem to reflect or echo passages from Dante.

John Greenleaf Whittier read, in translation, the *Inferno*, probably the *Paradise*, and at least part of the *New Life*. He wa strongly impressed by the beauty and charm of the *New Life*. In his prose writings Whittier referred to Dante or his work several times, and quoted from the *Inferno* once and the *New Life* once. And he mentioned Dante in five of his poems.

Oliver Wendell Holmes studied Italian in college, and read at least the *Inferno* by 1828. At some time he read at least part of the *Paradiso*. He acquired two Italian editions of the *Commedia* and four translations. In his prose writings there are about fifteen Dante references and a few quotations and echoes; in several letters he spoke of the translations by his friends Parsons and Longfellow; and in 1881 he sent to Florence, for a Dante meeting, a poem entitled "Boston to Florence." The poem closes with these lines addressed to Dante:

> Now to all lands thy deep-toned voice is dear,
> And every language knows the Song Divine!

In Edgar Allan Poe's writings between 1835 and 1850 there are sixteen Dante references and three quotations. And there are five instances of resemblance between passages in Poe's writings and passages in Dante — in one poem, one book review, and three stories. These passages seem to indicate that Poe knew the Ugolino story, Cantos I and V of the *Inferno*, and Dante's description of the forest of suicides, of the circle of burning sand, of the valley of serpents, and of the entrance to the City of Dis. He probably read the *Inferno* in Cary's translation, but his appreciation of Dante was apparently less profound than that of most other major American authors of the time.

Henry Thoreau, like Holmes, studied Italian at Harvard, read the *Inferno* there, at least by 1837, and acquired a copy of the *Commedia*. In his writings one finds sixteen references to Dante: some are general, a few refer to matters in the *Inferno*, and one mentions the P*aradise*.

Herman Melville bought a copy of Cary's "Dante" in 1848 and read the *Inferno* by the next year. And in his writings dating from 1849 on, there are more than a dozen Dante references. He refers, for example, to the inscription over the gate of Hell, to the story of Francesca, to the City of Dis, the story of Agnello, and the Phlegethon. He makes considerable use of Dante in the story *Pierre*. Although Melville was too much inclined to see in the *Inferno* the spirit of pessimism and revenge, he was also strongly impressed by the poem's truth to human experience, by its vividness and power, by some of its allegory, and by Dante's tenderness and spirit of aspiration. And Melville's interest was great enough for him to reflect it in ten of his works.

Walt Whitman read John Carlyle's translation of the *Inferno* in 1859 and wrote down his impressions of it. He especially remarked the work's intense brevity, great vigor, simple convincing realism and fascination as a well-told tragedy. Whitman kept this Carlyle translation to the end of his life, and read in it often. In three of his poems and in other pieces of his writing, one finds about twenty Dante references. He also looked over Dore's illustrations, and owned a copy of the Arundel Society's print of the Giotto portrait. And he admired Dante as a man who stood for the supreme ideals.

Our review reaches its climax with Henry Wadsworth Longfellow and James Russell Lowell.

Longfellow began reading the *Inferno* in Italian in 1828, and continued to read Dante's works for the rest of his life, a period of over fifty years. He wrote an essay on Dante in 1838, he taught a course in Dante at Harvard for sixteen years, he translated the *Commedia* (the first volume,

*Inferno*, was sent to Italy in 1865 for the anniversary celebration), and he wrote and compiled notes for his translation. In his letters, journals, and other works there are dozens of quotations from and references to Dante. In *Hyperion* and *Kavanagh* there are at least six passages influenced by parts of the *Commedia*. And twenty of his poems show Dantean influence.

The outstanding examples, of course, of Dantean influence on his poems are to be seen in his sonnet on "Dante" (published in 1845) and his six *Divina Commedia* sonnets (written in the 1860s). These poems not only are among the best of Longfellow's poems, but also are among the finest literary tributes which America at any time has paid to the Italian poet.

One of these is addressed directly to Dante.

O star of morning and of liberty!
O bringer of the light, whose splendor shines
Above the darkness of the Apennines,
Forerunner of the day that is to be!
The voices of the city and the sea,
The voices of the mountains and the pines,
Repeat thy song, till the familiar lines
Are footpaths for the thought of Italy!
Thy fame is blown abroad from all the heights,
Through all the nations, and a sound is heard,
As of a mighty wind, and men devout,
Strangers of Rome, and the new proselytes,
In their own language hear thy wondrous word,
And many are amazed and many doubt..

Lowell, like Thoreau and Holmes, began reading the *Inferno* while a student at Harvard, and for Lowell it was in the year 1836-37. About the same time, too, he began making references to Dante in his writing. After Longfellow's retirement from teaching, Lowell taught the Dante course at Harvard for twenty years. He also followed with great interest the translating being done by his friends Parsons, Longfellow, and Norton. And for the last nine years of his life he was President of the [American} Dante Society. Most important, for our purposes, he wrote a famous essay on Dante, which shows that his knowledge and appreciation of Dante's work was extensive, profound, and rich; and among his poems there are ten which show Dantean influence. But his greatest literary contribution to the Dante tradition in the United States was his essay.

This brings us to a convenient stopping place. Lowell died in 1891, approximately a century after the birth of America's interest in Dante. And by that time the interest was so firmly and permanently established that it has continued to grow ever since.

> *J. CHESLEY MATHEWS, Professor of English (Emeritus) in the University of California, Santa Barbara, is a graduate of Furman University, Duke University, and the University of California, Berkeley. He has taught courses in American literature and* The Divine Comedy. *In 1938, he was awarded the Harvard University Dante Prize. Professor Mathews served as Vice-President of AATI (1952), Chairman of the English Department of UC/SB (1951-1956), Fulbright Lecturer in American Literature at the University of Turin/Italy (1958-1959), consulting editor of* Italica *(1967-1968), Council Associate of The Dante Society of America (1971-1975). In 1976 he was honored with the title "Cavaliere" in the Italian Republic's Order of Merit. A member of MLA since 1935 and of The Dante Society and AATI since 1938, Professor Mathews has edited Ralph Waldo Emerson's translation of the* Vita Nuova *and has written many essays which trace the interest in Dante shown by various American authors.*

## Two Visions of the Journey of Life: Dante as Guide for Eliot and Pound

### James J. Wilhelm

In September of 1914, two young Americans who would change the entire course of twentieth-century poetry met in London for the first time.[1] They were T. S. Eliot and Ezra Pound. Despite some very basic differences in temperament, these expatriates-to-be had some strong common bonds: they were passionately devoted to the study of literature, and they were determined in their own ways to purify the English language of its post-romantic excesses and thus forge a viable new poetic idiom. The writer who probably exerted the greatest influence shared by both was Dante Alighieri.

This paper will deal with Dante's rhetorical influences and then concentrate on the larger problem of life goals or intellectual aims. With respect to rhetoric, both poets had studied the Italian in college: Pound at Hamilton and Eliot at Harvard. Both had been aware of Dante's greatness from the start. Pound wrote to his mother while at school: "Find me . . . a phenomenon of any importance in the lives of men and nations that you cannot measure with the rod of Dante's allegory."[2] Eliot acknowledged his debt in his criticism, especially when he made the much-quoted statement: "Dante and Shakespeare divide the modern world between them; there is no third."[3]

Although the Dantesque influence is apparent in the work of both, it has not been stressed in the formation of imagism through Pound.[4] It is clear from his first book of criticism, *The Spirit of Romance*, that Pound saw the author of the *Comedy* in the same light that he viewed the Greco-Roman classics and the Chinese written character as inspirations for verbal precision. Pound notes that Dante "says, not 'where a river pools itself,' but 'As at Arles, where the Rhone pools itself.'"[5] When Pound said of that first meeting with Eliot: "He is the only American I know of who has made what I can call adequate preparation for writing,"[6] Eliot's acquaintance with Italian literature — though not necessarily the language — was a major factor in their friendship.[7] Many years later, Pound paid Eliot the supreme compliment by saying, "His was the true Dantescan voice."[8] This was recompense for the great tribute that Eliot had given him earlier when he dedicated *The Waste Land* to Pound as *il miglior fabbro*.[9]

From the start, then, Dante was on their minds and in their poems. It would be pointless to indicate direct citations, since this has already been done numerous times.[10] Instead, this paper will concentrate on the more difficult question of how one writer can influence others in the planning and execution of their careers. Here I shall take recourse to the underlying rhythm of the *Comedy* — that of hellish immersion, purgatorial learning, and paradisal tranquility — in an attempt to find parallels in the two writers' works.

The infernal factor is perhaps the easiest to define. In their youths in London, where both men were struggling to survive — Eliot in a bank and Pound by doing hack journalistic work — Dante's Hell was all too real to both. Indeed, *The Waste Land* may be viewed in one way as a modern version of an Inferno, especially in such scenes as the one where Eliot describes the pale London office workers streaming across a bridge in the morning fog, modeling them after the aimless movements of the Trimmers in Inferno 3.55-57:

> Under the brown fog of a winter dawn,
> A crowd flowed over London Bridge, so many,
> I had not thought death had undone so many.[11]

Or again, in describing the tawdry life of a London secretary, he adapted Dante's haunting line on the tragic death of La Pia — *Siena mi fè, disfecemi Maremma* — into the memorable "Highbury bore me. Richmond and Kew / Undid me."[12] Eliot shows a true genius in his ability to take a Dantesque line and shape it into his own.

Pound also uses Dante in his Hell Cantos (14 and 15), but his uses there seem bookish. He scatters Italian phrases through his Early Cantos, and he appropriates the same line about La Pia, but merely drops it down as a subtitle for one of the parts of his farewell to London, *Hugh Selwyn Mauberley*.[13] This is imitation without adaptation. But the Pound of World War I days was an angry young man, outraged over social injustices. He was too preoccupied with things like usury to catch the quiet yet frustrated, detached yet morally assertive quality that Eliot captured so well.

After 1922; when *The Waste Land* had appeared and Pound had abandoned London for Paris and Rapallo, the two men entered a second stage of development. I shall call this a purgatorial phase, following Dante. In Eliot's case, his next writings — "The Hollow Men," "Ash Wednesday," and "The Rock" — clearly show the struggle of a soul to believe, and that is one fully valid definition of Purgatory. Since Eliot, in fact, converted to Anglicanism in 1927, his career can be traced along standard lines of spiritual development much more clearly than Pound's can. In fact, Eliot's fulfillment in writing *Four Quartets* shows the power of Christian meditation in act.

At this point, we shall leave Eliot to concentrate upon his friend, who had gone a different way into Mussolini's Italy. In the late twenties and the thirties Pound was as unorthodox a Christian as one could imagine. He was far more interested in a Confucian Earthly Paradise than a celestial one; he was deeply involved in economics and politics; and he frankly shows a greater fascination for the eccentric Guido Cavalcanti, whom he translated and adapted, than for Alighieri. So while Eliot was moving ever closer to Dante — no longer having to employ any suspension of disbelief in order to appreciate him[14] — Pound was drifting away from standard values, especially those of his native land. Yet curiously it was *he*, rather than Eliot, who wanted to write the great new epic of judgment for the modern world, as his title, *The Cantos*, indicates.

How could Pound follow Dante's general scheme without espousing the man's theology? The modern poet was all too well aware of the problem. He wrote in a letter: "Stage set *a la* Dante is *not* modern truth,"[15] and again and again he deplored the influence of Aquinas. The fact that Dante haunted him shows in his later statement that he had to keep searching for an epic form that would work, that was "elastic enough to take the necessary material"; and what was this material? — that which "wasn't in the *Divina Commedia*.[16] Furthermore, the triadic rhythm of Dante would not leave him, even though Pound thought of Hell, Purgatory, and Heaven as states of mind, not actual places.[17] Ultimately he settled on a musical form resembling a Bach fugue, in which statements could be made in three ways: some themes would be stated and abandoned, some would recur in different forms, and some would be permanent.[18]

The first kind of movement, which is wild and disordered, can be viewed as hellish; this is, to use the language of Richard of St. Victor, cogitation or the mind flitting aimlessly around an object. The second movement is the mind studying an object; this is meditation. The last, and highest form of thought is contemplation, where the mind and the object are one. And so Dante's great divisions of the Kingdom Beyond became in Pound's modern poem three states of mind that are constantly flowing. By definition, then, Purgatory to Pound has nothing to do with Christianity; it is a condition of learning, study, observation. Thus, his Middle Cantos, which were written largely in the Italy of the thirties, ignore Christian purgation totally and concentrate on doers: the Founding Fathers of America, the great Chinese despots, and the intelligent planners of the Bank of Siena. Instead of climbing a

## Two Visions of the Journey of Life: Eliot and Pound

mountain with Dante and Eliot, Pound wanted to build a Monte dei Paschi bank. But as fate would have it, neither he nor Mussolini could effect their Earthly Paradise, and the poet wound up in an animal cage in a detention camp at Pisa.

At this point in 1945, with the writing of *The Pisan Cantos*, Pound became emotionally involved in his life's work; this stretch of his poem is his true Purgatory. Stripped of most of his books, he becomes himself; moving out of past voices, he finds his own:

> What thou lovest well remains,
>         the rest is dross
> What thou lov'st well shall not be reft from thee.[19]

If his Purgatory is not Christian in a standard sense, it is nevertheless there as the poet identifies with the humblest forces of nature:

> When the mind swings by a grass-blade
>      an ant's forefoot shall save you.[20]

Acting now like the proud sinners groveling but finding true prayer in their round of Mount Purgatory, he proclaims a timeless piety:

> If the hoar frost grip thy tent
> Thou wilt give thanks when night is spent.[21]

Having carried the two poets through World War II, we can now mention the last phases of their careers, when both found peace in old age. Most critics, especially poets like Stephen Spender, believe that Eliot wrote his most accomplished work in the midst of the London blitzkrieg. Spender would point to such passages as the description of an encounter with a ghostly figure after an air-raid in *Little Gidding* — a passage, as Eliot tells us himself, that is modeled after Dante's *terza rima*, and, even though it lacks end rhymes, shows a marvelous ability to capture sustained thought in a continuously flowing language:[22]

> I caught the sudden look of some dead master

> Whom I had known, forgotten, half recalled
> Both one and many; in the brown baked features
> The eyes of a familiar compound ghost . . . .

The ghost then speaks about rage and guilt and shame, and tells how:

> . . . "fools' approval stings, and honour stains.
> From wrong to wrong the exasperated spirit
> Proceeds, unless restored by that refining fire
> Where you must move in measure, like a dancer."

Aside from the Dantesque cast to the rhythm and diction, the references to Brunetto Latini and Arnaut Daniel are obvious, while the ghost himself sounds a bit like Yeats and even, possibly, the refractory Pound.[23]

After the war, Eliot's years were filled with blessings. He gained a compatible wife, fame as a poet, success as a publisher, and the respect of even those who found it hard at times to overlook his propriety and rigidity. Pound, once again, had a tougher time: after Pisa came the long incarceration in the insane asylum in Washington. Vilified by many as a traitor, he had to settle for broken moments of joy, this passage that owes much to Dante indicates:[24]

> And from far
> 　　　il tremolar della marina
> chh chh
> 　　the pebbles turn with the wave
> chh ch'u
> 　　　"fui chiamat'
> 　　　　e qui refulgo"
> Le Paradis n'est pas artificiel
> 　　　　but is jagged,
> For a flash,
> 　　for an hour,
> 　　　　then agony,
> Hilary stumbles, but the Divine Mind is abundant
> 　　unceasing
> 　　　*improvisatore.*

Tragically true to his own preconceived design, Pound

could not enjoy lasting peace of mind. When he was at last allowed to return to Italy, he fell into a deep, a profound silence. When he bothered to speak to others at all, he was incredibly humble, saying that he was only a minor satirist whose work had come to nothing.[25] However, many critics feel that his last poetry, which was fashioned out of his suffering, is comparable with the later passionate, dissonant but still comprehensible work of Stravinsky.

Unlike Eliot, who writes sustained poetry conveying logically developed thought in a form consciously reminiscent of Beethoven's quartets, Pound excels in making sharp, staccato statements that rise out of the whirl of miasmic thought: "The temple is holy because it is not for sale."[26] If Eliot captures the flow of Dante's vision, Pound rearranges images and ideas in striking new patterns, as when he follows the Egyptian Kati in saying: "A man's paradise is his good nature."[27]

It is difficult to speak of two poets like these without making comparisons. They were friends in 1914 and, despite a certain rivalry, they were friends when Eliot died in 1965. In fact, the aged Pound even flew to London, and he wrote as a tribute that, with Eliot gone, "who is there now for me to share a joke with?"[28] That ability to be aware of comedy in the broadest sense in the midst of tragedy is but another way in which all three of these poets are united. On the occasion of this bicentennial celebration, we should not ask ourselves which poet Dante himself would prefer. Dante would undoubtedly thank them both for keeping significant expression alive, each according to his nature. Surely Dante would approve of Eliot's saying that the two words that one finds in his *Divine Comedy* that one cannot find substantively in the *Aeneid* are: *lume* and *amore*.[29] It is precisely that feeling of illumination and love that unites these two modern poets in their later work and that makes them both part of a great tradition that can be traced directly back to that earlier expert in sin, suffering, and salvation, Dante Alighieri.

## NOTES

The works of Ezra Pound are reprinted with the permission of New Directions Inc. of New York City and Faber and Faber of London; the works of Eliot are reprinted with the permission of Faber and Faber; and of Harcourt, Brace Jovanovich, Inc. of New York.

1. Biographical details from Noel Stock, *Life of Ezra Pound* (New York; Pantheon, 1970), p. 166.
2. Stock, p. 20.
3. "Dante," *Selected Essays* (New York: Harcourt, Brace, 1950), p. 225.
4. See my *Dante and Pound* (Orono: U. of Maine, 1974), pp. 27-41.
5. *The Spirit of Romance*, rev. ed. (New York: New Directions, n.d.), p. 159; 1st ed., 1910.
6. *The Letters of Ezra Pound 1907-1941*, ed. D. D. Paige (New York: Harcourt, Brace and World, 1950), p. 40; Sept. 30 to Harriet Monroe.
7. Eliot summarizes his education in "What Dante Means to Me," *To Criticize the Critic* (London: Faber and Faber, 1965), pp. 125-35. Cf. Mario Praz, "T. S. Eliot and Dante," *Southern Review*, 2 (1937), 525-48, who gives much credit to Pound.
8. "For T. S. E.," *Sewanee Review*, 74 (1966), 109.
9. *Purgatorio* 26.117; Eliot added the *il*.
10. My *Dante and Pound* lists earlier critics; see Grover Smith, *T. S. Eliot's Poetry and Plays* (Chicago: U. of Chicago, 1956), pp. 147-57 et al.; also, Praz, see n. 7.
11. *The Waste Land*, lines 61-63, in *Complete Poems and Plays 1909-1950* (New York: Harcourt, Brace and World, 1971), p. 39.
12. *The Waste Land*, lines 293-94, p. 46; based on *Purgatorio* 5.1.33.
13. *Personae* (New York: New Directions, 1926), p. 193.
14. "Dante," p. 219.
15. *Letters*, p. 293; 1937 to John Lackay Brown.
16. Donald Hall, "Ezra Pound: An Interview," *Paris Review*, 28 (1962), 23.24.
17. *Spirit of Romance*, p. 128; cf Eliot, "Dante," p. 21.

18. *Dante and Pound*, pp. 50, 54-56.
19. Canto 81, pp. 520f., in *The Cantos* (New York: New Directions, 1972).
20. Canto 83, p. 533.
21. Canto 84, p. 540.
22. *Complete Poems and Plays*, pp. 140,142; see Stephen Spender, *T. S: Eliot* (New York: Viking, 1976), pp. 179-84.
23. See Graham Rough, "Dante and Eliot," *Critical Quarterly. 16* (1974), pp. 293-305. An excellent analysis and comparison with Pound is to be found in Glauco Cambon's "Dante's Presence in American Literature," *Dante's Craft* (Minneapolis: University of Minnesota, 1969), pp. 119-145, esp. pp. 139-143.
24. Canto 92, p. 620.
25. Michael Reck. "A Conversation Between Ezra Pound and Allen Ginsberg," *Evergreen Review, 55* (1968), 27; also, C. David Heymann, *Ezra Pound; The Last Rower* (New York: Viking, 1976), pp. 272ff.
26. Canto 97, p. 697 et al.
27. Canto 93, p. 623.
28. "For T. S. E.," 109.
29. "Virgil and the Christian World," *On Poetry and Poets* (New York: Farrar, Straus and Cudahy. 1957), p. 147.

> *JAMES J. WILHELM is Pofessor of Comparative Literature at Rutgers Univerisity. Born in Youngstown, Ohio, on February 2, 1932, he was educated at the University of Bologna and Yale University, where he received the Ph.D. in 1961. He has taught since 1966 at Rutgers. Wilhelm is the author of numerous articles on medieval and modern literature. His books include* The Cruelest Month: Spring, Nature and Love in Classical and Medieval Lyrics *(Yale),* Seven Troubadours *(Penn State),* Medieval Song *(Dutton),* Dante and Pound *(Maine),* The Later Cantos of Ezra Pound *(Walker & Co. of New York).*

DANTE ON GALWAY KINNELL'S
"LAST RIVER"

GLAUCO CAMBON

With *Body Rags* of 1968,[1] Galway Kinnell — one of the best American poets in the post-World-War-II generation — resumed the epic bent of his first book, *What a Kingdom It Was*.[2] There, his lyrical vocation had clearly broadened its scope to epic amplitude in sustained pieces like "The Avenue Bearing the Initial of Christ Into the New World," a colorful pageant of New York street life, or like "Easter,"[3] a commentary on present-day listlessness and violence in the guise of a striking descant on Catholic liturgy, or several lyrics that I once happened to call "notes toward an American epic" because they captured in their crisp idiom the vistas of a vanished frontier. In the 1969 collection, Kinnell's critical attitude toward industrial America went hand in hand with an undampened alertness for the sensory richness of a nature threatened by the man-made blight we all have come to dread, and his lucid, supple and vivid style, equally immune to academic complacency and anti-intellectual formlessness, stood him in good stead for the task of mirroring his own political and existential concerns in Dante's prophetic vision. If "The Last River,"[4] the longest poem in *Body Rags*, freely structures itself on *Inferno*, it is more than a matter of quotations and framing references; it amounts, on the part of the modern American poet, to a recognition of affinity between his own mode of perception and the medieval Florentine's mode. This can hardly surprise any reader of Eliot, Yeats and Pound, of Lowell and Tate and Snodgrass,[5] namely of the twentieth-century British and American poets who have variously come to terms with the Dantean example of poetry as criticism of life. Even such a radical rejector of Western "white" culture as LeRoi Jones, lately rebaptized Imamu Baraka, had to pattern his own searing autobiography — the story of a youth tossed between two incompatible worlds in the infernal urban scene of today's America — on "the system of Dante's Hell."[6]

In Galway Kinnell's case, too, the Dantean cue serves to focus an autobiographical stance into a critical act which encompasses contemporary America and its involved observer in its very midst. Like Dante, Galway is both actor and spectator, both character and literary witness in his visionary narrative, and like Dante again, he names himself only once, at a crucial point, in a poem that keeps saying "I." For Dante this branding identification comes on the summit of Purgatory, when Beatrice (Canto XXX, lines 55-57) disabusingly upbraids him at the very time he thinks he has left all shameful burdens behind:

> "Dante, just because Virgil is now leaving
> Do not cry yet, oh no, do not yet cry;
> Another wound will give you cause to cry."[7]

For Galway Kinnell, the same ordeal comes toward the end of his persona's pilgrimage, in Stanza 26 (they are 27 in all), when in the prison cell that has provided the defining ambience and starting point for his mind trip

> the light goes out. In the darkness
> a letter for the blind
> arrives in my stunned hands.
> Did I come all this way only for this, only
> to feel out the world-braille of my complicity,
> only to choke down these last poison wafers?
> *For Galway alone.*
> *I send you my mortality.*
> *Which leans out from itself, to spit on itself.*
> *Which you would not touch.*
> *All you have known.*

In both symbolic autobiographies, the cruel act of naming — a baptism of fire — does not come from the speaking "I" but from an imperious entity with parental implications that forces the autobiographical persona to the wall. Self-judgment is thus objectively extracted from the judging self who had passed judgment on the sinners of this world in an epic review, respectively, of thirteenth-century Europe and twentieth- century America.

But if for Dante this last humiliation, this baptism of fire, signals the final purging and so ushers in the new baptism by immersion in the waters of Lethe, river of blessed oblivion, for Galway the sequel is uncertain and in fact ominous. Dante's last rivers are the one that cleanses him of any memory of sins committed (Lethe ) and the one that restores memory of good deeds (Eunoe), while Kinnell's last river, as described in St. 25 and again in St. 27, the final stanza, is a combination of Lethe and Styx:

> We come to a river
> where many thousands kneel, sucking up
> its cloudy water
> in a kind of frenzy . . .
> "What river is it?" I ask.
> "The Mystic River," Henry David says,
> "the Healing Stream free to all
> that flows from Calvary's Mountain . . . the liquor
> that makes you forget . . . ." (St. 25, beginning)
> On one bank
> of the last river stands
> a black man, on the other
> a white man, on the water between
> a man of no color,
> body of beryl,
> face of lightning,
> eyes lamps of wildfire,
> arms and feet of polished brass.

> *There will come an agony upon you*
> *beyond any*
> *this nation has known;*
> *and at that time thy people,*
> *given intelligence, given imagination, given love,/given . . .*

> Here his voice falters, he drops
> to his knees, he is
> falling to pieces,
> no nose left,
> no hair,
> no teeth,
> limbs dangling from prayer-knots and rags,
> Waiting by the grief-tree
> of the last river. (St. 17)

The italicized parts of St. 26 and St. 27 sum up respectively a personal revelation to the self who is undergoing purgation (Galway) and to the whole nation that includes him (aptly polarized into black and white to spotlight its ethnic and inner dissociation). Despite obvious differences, this sequence of messages parallels the much vaster one to be heard in Cantos XXX to XXXII of Dante's *Purgatorio*, where Beatrice first wrings contrition from Dante to release in him the wellspring that will wash away his residual impurity, and then shows him the apocalyptic charade that will be her coded message on the awful decay of Church and Empire, to be expressly reported by him in his verse as a warning to deviant Christianity:

> "Here you will be for a short while a forest dweller,
> And with me you will be a citizen forever
> Of that Rome whereof Christ himself is Roman.
> But now, for the sake of the world that so ill lives,
> Do keep your eyes fixed on the chariot, and
> Once you're back down there, write what you have
> seen."     (*Purg.* XXXII, 100-105)

In both the Italian and the American poem we thus have a transition from an excruciating personal message to a no less excruciating public one of prophetic import, which in Dante's case amounts to an explicit investiture of vatic functions while in Kinnell's case it remains on the level of a shattering experience followed by no ritual sanctioning. The modern poet has no transcendent source to validate his revelation, and indeed his apocalyptic message comes first in total darkness, from an unidentified if strangely intimate personal source (St. 26), and then from a nightmarish father figure that pointedly recalls the composite statue of Daniel's vision and of *Inferno* XIV (the Old Man of Crete) but is subsequently reduced to a fast disintegrating corpse (St. 2.7). Instead of preparing the poet persona for a vatic mission and a successful ascent to Heaven, the kaleidoscopic disclosure of trouble seems to leave Galway in a still quasi-infernal predicament, as witness the fact that blindness and closure are the ambience, and murkiness and decay the vision. The final outcome is in doubt, and the possibility of hope is not ruled out, but the emphasis is on present horror and precariousness. Far from receiving from his guide the assurance of a paradisal liberation, the pilgrim persona here is left with the frightening prospect of a plunge back into deepest hell; in fact there is no guide once the shock of revelation has come, and whether contemporary America, the pilgrim's home, will turn out to be a no-exit trap or a community capable of choosing its better future through the ordeal of a purgatorial soul-searching, remains appropriately undecided.

Kinnell's Catholic upbringing has undoubtedly concurred with his literary expertise in orienting him on Dante's *Inferno* and *Purgatorio* as the aptest model for his own poetical act of individual and communal purgation, but the chosen model has elicited from the American poet what was most uniquely his. Kinnell has used Dante instead of being used by him, and what Virgil as a literary source was to the medieval poet, the medieval poet in turn has been to Kinnell — self-recognition in the formidable literary ancestor being for Kinnell a necessary part of his own self-differentiation. There is of course a Virgil in Kinnell's poem; he appears in Stanza 15, "out of the mist," and he takes Galway's hand to "lead [him] over the plain of crushed asphodel," giving his own name as "Henry David": who but Thoreau the lover of unspoiled nature and antiwar protester could have guided his modern fellow writer through the circles of the unbeautiful and the damned which, in Kinnell's nightmarish vision, seem to make up the contemporary American scene? And as our bewildered wayfarer, under his newfangled Virgil's guidance, reviews the several stations of his nightmare, meeting the filth and despair of political corruption, chicanery, violence, social neglect and philistinism, precise *Inferno* references pinpoint the moral judgment along with the literary ancestry which supports that judgment. St. 17 depicts a Charon-like ferryman, "at water's edge,/oar in hand, kneeling beside/his pirogue of blue stern . . . ," then exposes us to "the threshold groan" reminiscent of the wailing and howling that hits Dante's ears upon crossing Hell's gate in *Inferno* III, only that here the eerie noise comes from "the pressurized/bayou water" squirting in "at the seams" of the boat "in the patches free of scum"; St. 21 again quotes from *Inferno* III to castigate contemporary Americans in positions of power who behaved like Dante's uncommitted angels and neutral sinners by dodging their moral responsibilities:

> We come to a crowd, hornets
> in their hair, worms in their feet.
> "They weren't for anything or against anything,"
> Henry David says, "they looked out
> for themselves."

(Thoreau himself was notoriously untainted by this weakness; he is after all the author of *Civil Disobedience*.) St. 22 lashes out at the brutishness of the pampered classes by making one of their members utter the nonsensical gibberish Dante puts on the lips of chained giant Nimrod, the Babelic perverter of language, in *Inferno* XXXI: "*Raphel may amech zabi almi*." St. 23 deftly evokes the logician devil of *Inferno* XXVII, who outwitted Guido da Montefeltro the evil counselor of Pope Boniface, in order to expose the doubletalk and self-deception of such articulate liberals as do not practice what they preach:

> "That one,"
> says my guide, "was

well-meaning; he believed
in equality and supported the good causes;
he got a shock, when he found out
this place is run by logicians . . . ."

The Dantesque nightmare reaches an unforeseen climax when the victims of violence themselves appear to the pilgrim (St. 24) and when (St. 26) the national conscience (Galway's avowed "hero") materializes as a compound figure with Thoreauvian, Altgeldian, and even Schweitzerian traits*, to denounce in his own symbolic person the ethical limitations of some of the best in America's heritage of conduct: love of purity for one's own selfish sake, a painful recognition for the child of a country where Puritanism remains an unignorable mainspring of behavior.

Searchingly unpredictable as they are, the two conclusive stanzas presuppose the whole poem in its fluvial unfolding from the prison cell-block reverie (punctuated by shrill reminders of the actual situation the persona is forced to share with common criminals), through his memories of a wondering childhood and free adolescence somehow spent always on or in sight of rivers, to the insistent Dantesque references that, beginning with Stanza 16, structure memory into vision and vision into judgment. Like Dante himself, Kinnell draws on a personal experience with traumatic as well as uplifting implications that make for an apocalyptic rather than just deftly literary outcome in the encounter with the venerable source. Just as Dante finds his freedom and salvation by confronting Hell's claustrophobia to re-emerge into the open starlit spaces from a narrow tunnel crawling through earth's bowels, Galway finds his freedom in a dark jail, "liberty . . . being/brightest in dungeons"[9]; and then it is an exhilaratingly free voice that surges forward to recapitulate the persona's American childhood and *Wanderjahre*:

And putting on again
its skin of light, the river
bends into view. We watch it, rising

between the levees, flooding for the sky. (St. 11)

All my life, of rivers
I hear
the longing cries, rut-roar
of shifted wind
on the gongs of beaten water . . .

the Ten Mile of Hornpout,
the Drac hissing in its bed of sand,
the Ruknabad crossed by ghosts of nightingales,
the Passumpsic bursting down its length in
   spring . . . . (St. 14)

The ravages inflicted by shortsighted greed, Dante's she-wolf, cannot be fully realized by the American poet unless he brings into his picture the contrapuntal luxuriance and vastness of what was, and could still be, unraped America, the America Thoreau, Whitman and Twain knew. That vastness dawns on the persona within the walls of a Southern prison where he has been thrown — along with thieves, pimps and their likes — for trying to help the local black citizens to register as voters. Dante's example has acted as a liberating, not as a constraining force, for the *engagé* poet trying to comprehend his experience in its social context.

And it is not inappropriate to add that the same catalytic energy makes itself felt in Galway Kinnell's style. Though he writes free verse and stanzas m the manner of Whitman and Pound, not *terza rima*, his sharp eye for detail, his sense of the specific weight of things in the world, and his mimetic use of rhythm through expressive continuities and discontinuities, do amount to a marked affinity for Dante's severe eloquence — that eloquence which helped him to decipher the world of fact in the light of apocalypse, and now well serves Kinnell in the effort to penetrate the opacity of contemporary history with the X-rays of ethical values. Of such feeling for tangible, individualized reality, and of the concomitant ability to make it transparent to the mind's eye, already the first stanza of "The Last River" provides an adequate sample, so that it will aptly close our voyage, as readers, all the way upstream:

> When I cross
> on the high, back-reared ferry boat
> all burnished brass and laboring pistons
> and look at the little tugs and sticklighters
> and the great ships from foreign lands
> and wave to a deckhand gawking at the new world
> of sugar cans and shanties and junked cars
> and see a girl by the ferry rail,
> the curve the breeze makes down her thigh,
> and the green waves lighting up . . .
> the cell-block
> door crawls open and they fling us a pimp.

Going all the way upstream, in this case, means for us readers temporarily to invert the normal course; and if by this inversion of route on "The Last River" we happen to find ourselves, not at the source, but at the mouth of the Mississippi, crowded with the accruals and debris of modern industrial civilization, we shall be better placed to start again, with the poem's speaker, on the never ending quest for that source which is both at the beginning and at the end of life's troublesome river.

NOTES

1. Galway Kinnell: *Body Rags* (Boston: Houghton Mifflin, 1968, London: Rapp & Whiting, Poetry USA Series, 7. 1969).

2. Galway Kinnell: *What a Kingdom It Was* (Boston: Houghton Mifflin, 1960).

3. For a detailed analysis of that poem, which is clearly germane to our present topic, see my discussion of Kinnell's first book, pp. 30-36 of *Recent American Poetry* (University of Minnesota Pamphlets on American Writers No. 16, Minneapolis, Minn. 1962). For another, and more extensive study of Kinnell's poetry (including "Easter"), see Ralph J. Mills, Jr., "A Reading of Galway Kinnell" (*The Iowa Review* 1/1, Winter 1970, pp. 66-86).

4. *Body Rags* pp. 33-49.

5. W. D. Snodgrass: *In Radical Pursuit*, part III, "Four Studies in the Classics," including "Analysis of Depths: *The Inferno*" pp. 275-319 (New York: Harper & Row, 1975). This essay (originally published in 1969 and delivered as a lecture at the University of New Hampshire) shows how the lucid and incisive poet of *Heart's*

*Needle* (1969) can think and feel himself into the Dantean cosmos as part of his own catharsis-psychoanalysis supplying the clue.

6. LeRoi Jones: *The System of Dante's Hell* (New York: Grove Press, 1965).

7. "Dante, perché Virgilio se ne vada
non pianger anco, non piangere ancora;
ché pianger ti convien per altra spada."
Dante Alighieri, *La Commedia* secondo l'antica vulgata, a cura di Giorgio Petrocchi. Vol. 3, *Purgatorio*, p. 519 (Milan: Mondadori, 1967).

8. "Quì sarai tu poco tempo silvano;
e sarai meco sanza fine cive
di quella Roma onde Cristo è romano.
Però, in pro del mondo che mal vive,
al carro tieni or li occhi, e quel che vedi,
ritornato di là, fa che tu scrive."
Dante Alighieri, *La Commedia* secondo l'antica vulgata, cit., vol. 3, p. 561.

9. This quotation from Shelley occurs in Stanza 7.

(*) Unless the poet himself were willing to specify the reference, it will remain private. Since the figure in question appears with frontiersman trappings and speaks German ("mein Herz!"), he may well be Albert Bierstadt, the popular painter and pioneer of the West who emigrated from Germany. But this nineteenth century figure obviously enters the poem only as an emblematic type, coalescing with Thoreau, Buffalo Bill, and other representatives of the American frontier age.

> *GLAUCO CAMBON was visiting professor in English and American literature at the University of Michigan (Ann Arbor) before moving to Rutgers University as Professor of Comparative Literature and Romance Languages and later to the University of Connecticut (Storrs). Educated in Italy, Professor Cambon first came to the United States as a Fulbright Scholar (Columbia University). Later, he returned to Italy as a Fulbright Lecturer. His numerous publications include* The Inclusive Flame *(1963),* La Lotta con Proteo *(1963),* Recent American Poetry *(1962),* Ungaretti *(1967),* Dante's Craft *(1969), and scores of translations and articles.*

# PART THREE

## DANTE AND THE "QUEST FOR ELOQUENCE" IN INDIA'S VERNACULAR LANGUAGES

by

ANNE PAOLUCCI / HENRY PAOLUCCI

(From *Review of National Literatures*,
Volume 10, *India,*
Council on National Literatures,
Special Editor: RONALD WARWICK
[New York, 1979] pp. 70-144).

# DANTE AND THE "QUEST FOR ELOQUENCE" IN INDIA'S VERNACULAR LANGUAGES

"Vernacular" speech ... is the kind we learn without rules, simply by imitating. What the Romans called "grammar" is a second kind.... Of the two, the vernacular is nobler, for it is natural, while the other is artificial.
Dante, *On Eloquence in the Vernacular*, c. 1304-1309[1*].

Sanskrit is like the water of a deep well, but the vernacular is like a running brook.
Kabir, *The Seed Book*, c. 1500[2]

The average number of speakers per literary language [in South Asia] is greater than in Europe.... Hindi-Urdu, with 235 million speakers ranks as the fourth language in the world (after Mandarin Chinese, English, and Spanish, while Russian is fifth). Bengali, with 130 million speakers, is the sixth language. [Also] of numerical significance are Marathi with 50 million, Punjabi (47 million), Telugu (44 million), and Tamil (44 million). Kannada, Gujarati, Malayalam, and Uriya have 20 to 30 million each.
Clarence Maloney, "The Real Language Problem in South Asia," 1974[3]

Does modern India have a national author or canon of authors whose works can be said to have given its Indian identity a characteristically national literary expression? Is there, or has there been, a towering national poet or playwright like Dante, Shakespeare, or Goethe, or some group of peers, headed by Indian equivalents of Cervantes and Lope de Vega or Rabelais and Racine, whose artistic medium is a genuinely living Indian national language? What is the national literary language of modern India?

If the answer to that last question were Sanskrit — and there are still many scholars in India as well as in the

West who insist that it can only be Sanskrit — then it would be relatively easy to supply and document highly positive answers to the preceding questions. "The literary tradition of India," specialists in the field like to remind us, "goes back more than 3,000 years, and during the greater part of this time it was dominated by Sanskrit, first in its Vedic, and later in its classical form."[4] With Sanskrit as its national language, modern India could at once claim for itself a living literary legacy complete in all the major genres, lyric, epic, and dramatic.

Vedic Sanskrit offers us thousands of hymns, ritual texts, and richly-poetic philosophical treatises that have been compared to the most sublime songs of divine praise in the Hebrew *Old Testament* as well as to the cosmogonies and theogonies of the early Greek poets, including Hesiod, the georgic poems of Virgil, and even the *De Rerum Natura* of the pan-materialist Lucretius. In the grand epic sweep of its seemingly endless *Mahabharata* (of which the celebrated *Bhagavad-gita* is an episode) and the more disciplined *Ramayana*, post-Vedic Sanskrit represents for us "the Indian world view in all its splendor and magnificence, its confusion, its fantastic absurdity, and its dissolution."[5] It is a world view that surely bears comparison with what Homer achieves in the *Iliad* and the *Odyssey*. Indeed, just as, through many centuries, Greeks of every class drew spiritual sustenance from the Homeric poems, so it can be said that, "in the form of oral reading or recitation," India's two great epics — we cite here the words of the eminent Oxford Professor of Sanskrit, F. W. Thomas — "have been until modern times the main literary sustenance of the Indian masses" who have known them, if not in the original, at least in translations or adaptations of comparable fame, some in Indo-Aryan derivative vernaculars such as Bengali and Assamese, others in Dravidian vernaculars such as Kannada and Telugu.[6] And finally, in its truly classical form, Sanskrit offers us the exquisite refinement of the great Kalidasa, whose *Shakuntala* (translated by Sir William

Jones in 1789) quickly induced the Sanskrit playwright's new European admirers to hail him as the Shakespeare of India.

Yet, more than 1500 years have passed since Kalidasa's time — as long an interval as that which separated Rome's Cicero from Rotterdam's Latin-speaking and Latin-thinking Erasmus. Can it really be claimed that Sanskrit, which even in Kalidasa's age was not a language in common use, qualifies today as a living national language in the modern sense?

The modern case for Sanskrit is perhaps best summed up by Sanskrit Professor A. K. Warder of the University of Toronto in his chapter on the "Classical Literature" of India contributed to A. L. Basham's excellent *Cultural History of India* (1975). In the closing pages of that chapter, Professor Warder argues that India's classical Sanskrit tradition had managed to survive six hundred years of Muslim rule virtually intact because the Muslim conquerors had made no serious effort to penetrate its innermost sanctuaries of carefully-guarded purity. The British, helped by native collaborators, did violate those sanctuaries; and, according to Professor Warder, they went on to do much worse. "Under the British," he writes, "the Indian tradition was submerged by the imposition of English as medium of administration and education, except in the 'Native States' such as Travancor and Cochin. The modern vernaculars under this domination" — which is to say, no longer under the tutelage of Sanskrit — "partly copied European models and developed a hybrid literature which is neither European nor Indian." The end of British rule in 1947 might have made a difference; with governmental support, a revival of the submerged tradition might have been attempted. But instead, the English-educated leaders of the new Union of India persisted in the inherited British attitudes in education, so that now, as Professor Warder concludes:

... the unity of India is threatened by the centrifugal

force or the vernaculars. Vernacular writers often seek European orbits, considered "modern," lacking the national character and relationship among themselves which only the common Indian tradition could give them. Sanskrit is the only truly national language India has ever had, linking all regions and classes with the immortal springs of Indian thought. If it disappears, with its cultural heritage, India will never be a nation and will surely break up into a series of European-type states. The decision still lies in the future; meanwhile the semi-underground classical tradition conserves its vigour and the twentieth century has produced several hundred Sanskrit plays, whilst the theatre of Bhasa is being revived in Kerala. India's cultural unity may yet be saved and through it her political unity. ([4] 196)

For a perhaps clearer literary impression of how the classical Indian tradition of which Professor Warder speaks might have continued to function down into our time, had it not been submerged by British educational policy, we may turn to Professor J. A. B. van Buitenen's brief evocation in *The Literatures of India* (1974). Professor Buitenen there says of Sanskrit, first of all, that "the very name of the language, one of the few not derived from a region or a people, states its own program: *sanskrta bhasa* is the ritually perfected and intellectually cultivated language. If one is to speak the language, he must speak it correctly. It is the proud possession of one whose birth pre-disposes him to education." It is always an acquired, second language; but that makes it all the more a deliberately-cultivated rather than instinctive medium of communication, which permits its possessor to "speak to other educated Indians across the growing barriers between regionally developing dialects, and across the eternal barriers between the language families themselves."

Because of the long training required to master his "ritually perfected" language — hardly a language for Gandhi and his beloved *harijans*! — the accomplished Sanskrit-speaker would no doubt "take extraordinary delight in reproducing complex clusters of consonants that his regional vernacular might have lost," and in "drawing on a meta-vocabulary that his regional tongue could not supply." He would become, in effect, writes Buitenen, "an Erasmus conversing, through Latin and on things Latin, with a Thomas More, reserving his peasant Flemish for his maid and fellow villagers." But wouldn't such elevated, trans-regional Sanskrit discourse "result in a sometimes frustrating unconcern with specificity, with details of time, place, and person"? Do we not have here one of the inherent limitations — "limitations from at least one point of view" — of the classical Sanskrit tradition? Yes, writes Buitenen; but "to the speaker of Sanskrit" in the past, "they were not felt as limitations, for he also had his regional vernacular in which he could meaningfully discuss matters of everyday and be sure his fellow speaker, from the same region, would understand his references." ([2] 10-11)

The same point had been made by Sir Percival Spear back in 1948, shortly after independence, but with an entirely different emphasis. After a marvelously brief but accurate review of the variety of India's languages, in his *India, Pakistan, and the West,* he observed about Sanskrit that, "at one time it was thought to be the parent of all the Aryan languages, but it is now accepted as the sister of Greek and Latin, of ancient Persic and Avestic. As the [Aryan] invaders spread over Northern India the tribal dialects tended to develop into local languages; one of them thus became the Sanskrit language, which, standardized in the early Hindu scriptures, became first the speech of the polite, and then a dead language for priests and scholars. Learned men can still converse in Sanskrit as Renaissance scholars talked in Latin."[7]

Two years earlier, on the eve of British India's partition into a predominantly Hindu independent Union of India and a predominantly Muslim independent Pakistan, Jawaharlal Nehru published his widely-influential *Discovery of India* (1946), which devotes a central subchapter to "The Vitality and Persistence of Sanskrit." Writing as a political realist — indeed as the designated "political heir" of Mohandas K. Gandhi who is India's Mazzini, Cavour, and Garibaldi all rolled into one — Nehru acknowledged first of all that Sanskrit had in fact been a "dead language" in Sir Percival Spear's sense for a very long time, that "even in the days of Kalidasa it was not the people's language, though it was the language of educated people throughout India." As for its prospects as a possible all-India language of the future, the man who was soon to become the independent Union of India's first Prime Minister spoke with caution. He had noted that, despite its submergence during the Muslim centuries when even high-caste Brahmans cultivated Persian as the all-India language of the educated, Sanskrit had continued to display, within its narrowed sphere, a truly "amazing vitality." And then, with a political realist's manifestly sincere expression of gratitude for the kindly thought, he cited the view of the highly esteemed friend of India, Oxford Professor F. W. Thomas.

"Speaking at the Oriental Conference held in 1937 at Trivandrum, over which he presided," wrote Nehru,

> Dr. F. W. Thomas pointed out what a great unifying force Sanskrit had been in India and how widespread its use still was. He actually suggested that a simple form of Sanskrit, a kind of Basic Sanskrit, should be encouraged as a common all-India language today! He quoted, agreeing with him, what Max Müller had said previously: "Such is the marvelous continuity between the past and the present in India, that in spite of repeated social convulsions, religious reforms, and foreign invasions, Sanskrit may be said to be still the only language spoken over the whole extent of that vast country . . . . Even at the present moment, after a century of English rule and English teaching, I believe that Sanskrit is more widely understood in India than Latin was in Europe at the time of Dante."[8]

## 1. The Sanskrit Revival: From Comparative Linguistics to Classical Nostalgia

Friedrich "Max" Müller (1823-1900) was the most famous Sanskritist of the West in the late nineteenth century. A "British orientalist" by scholarly adoption, Müller had done his best to arouse an almost popular enthusiasm (often presenting himself in the guise of a publicist rather than a scholar) for what he called a "Renaissance of Sanskrit literature." Indeed, as the reference to Dante in the passage quoted implies, he had undertaken in effect to launch in behalf of Sanskrit the same sort of humanist crusade that Petrarch — "morning-star" of the European Renaissance — had launched in behalf of classical Latin shortly after the death of Dante in 1321.

Taken in context, the point of Müller's comparison of the status of Latin in Dante's Europe with that of Sanskrit in modern India is clear. How strong was Latin's position in Europe before Petrarch's time? It is a matter of historical record that, for more than a century before Dante wrote his *Commedia* in his native Florentine dialect, young poets all over Europe had been rejecting the use of the Latin of the Church as a literary language. It was too artificial, too overladen with scholastic abstractions, they seemed convinced, for the expression of intimate feelings; and, even worse, since it could only be learned by hard study, it remained for the most part unintelligible to the women, the *gentle ladies*, for whose eyes and hearts most of the new poetry was being written, whether in the new German of the Hohenstaufen imperial courts, or in Gallic Provençal or French, or in the many dialects of Italy.

Though he had been well-schooled in the Latin of his time, and though he knew the classical Latin poetry of Virgil, which he loved, literally by heart, Dante, as is well-known, had very early joined the ranks of the modernist or avantgarde poets who wrote in the vernaculars. And very early too he had chosen to burn his Latin bridges behind him, so to speak, by publishing a literary "manifesto" on the subject — his brilliantly-polemical Latin treatise "On Eloquence in the Vernacular": *De Vulgari Eloquentia* — where he defends his practice on several grounds, not the least of which was his unshakable conviction that history was on his side, that the linguistic-literary future of Europe lay not with Latin in any form but with the emergent national vernaculars.

It isn't easy to explain why, after Dante had made his case for the vernaculars and had produced his *Commedia* in validation of it, educated Europe should have spent the next two centuries trying desperately to obstruct that historical development. When Dante died, Petrarch was a youth of seventeen. He too had felt the need to write in his native Tuscan dialect to give adequate poetic expression to intimate feelings. But, unlike Dante, he had no confidence that the emergent vernaculars could ever provide a solid base for lasting literary fame. What sort of fame could even a Dante expect for himself, in the long run, by writing in a regionally-restricted, constantly-changing dialect which was understood in Italy by no more than a fraction of one percent of the population and by virtually no one outside of Italy? As Erich Auerbach observes, the most eminent humanists from Petrarch (1304-1374) to Sir Thomas More (1478-1535) and Erasmus (1466-1536) "were contemptuous of the Middle Ages, of scholastic philosophy, and of the Low Latin in which it was expressed"; yet their contempt for their contemporaries who turned to the vernaculars, contenting themselves with a "merely" French or English, or Italian fame, was even greater. Why encourage cultural fragmentation of a possibly irremediable kind by pursuing such a course? Since the "Latin of the priests" had in fact been allowed to fall so low in expressive capacity that talented poets refused to use it, then the obvious remedy, according to the humanists, was to set about undoing the linguistic damage of a "thousand barbarous years" by reviving the Latin of Cicero, Virgil, and Horace in its ancient classical purity. The Petrarchans, to quote Professor Auerbach once more, "wished to return to the great classics of the Golden Age of Latin literature," and so they "sought out the manuscripts of those classics, imitated their styles, and adopted their conception of literature, based on classical rhetoric."[9]

We thus return to the point of Max Müller's comparison. Though they tried hard to revive classical Latin, the European Renaissance humanists failed. But, in Müller's view, the reason they failed is obvious: they had started their revival from a wholly inadequate base. The inherited Latin of the Church had simply been allowed to sink too low. Nothing comparable, Müller is reminding us, has ever happened to classical Sanskrit. Sanskrit-Hindu India, quite like Latin-Christian Rome, had had its age of barbarism. It had come on the heels of the early Muslim invasions just a few centuries after the glorious time of Kalidasa. The Turkish Muslims who completed the conquest had a native speech so crude, in their own view, that for official use they early adopted a language as foreign to them, namely Persian, as to their Hindu subjects. Culturally, it was a situation quite like that of Western Roman Europe under its Germanic masters — with one essential difference. Through all the centuries under the Muslims, the priestly custodians of Sanskrit never permitted its use for mass preaching or teaching to win Hindu converts out of the ranks of the conquerors. In the West, on the contrary, once the ancient Church leaders decided to extend their "pastoral care" to the conquering tribes, their inherited Latin had immediately become a "mission" language. Before long, even the Latin-educated priesthood, which was not hereditary, came to be recruited out of the ranks of the new peoples, and then the last restraints on linguistic transformation gave way. Periodically, efforts were made to hold the line at least with respect to a few treasured texts of early Latin Christendom, like St. Jerome's Vulgate Bible for instance. But, as Giacomo Devoto aptly observes in his

*Languages of Italy* (1978), those very efforts were proof to scholar, priest, and layman alike that "biblical Latin was one thing and the Latin he believed he was speaking quite another. The latter was no longer Latin, though he still called Latin."[10]

When Islamic rule over Hindu India was finally ended in the second half of the eighteenth century, the British who ended it found in fact a linguistic-cultural situation quite the opposite of what had occurred in Roman Europe during the Middle Ages. Emancipated Hindu India had its regional vernaculars, to be sure: the languages actually spoken by the people, including a hybrid *lingua franca* that fused the Persian vocabulary of the ruling Muslims with one of the more widely diffused Hindu dialects. But there was no equivalent of the Low Latin of the medieval Christian Church. Before that time, the British had hardly been aware of the existence of classical Sanskrit; yet when it finally came to light, and they began to study it, the scholars among them were soon informed by its traditional priestly custodians that it was still quite the same language it had been when the great Kalidasa wrote his plays in it, centuries before the first Muslim invasions. Thus if a classical Sanskrit revival were ever attempted in India, the language, at any rate, would be ready at hand. Given the carefully-guarded purity of Sanskrit, simply to will what Petrarch willed might very well suffice, therefore, to achieve in India what two-hundred years of Herculean humanistic labor had failed to achieve for classical Latin in Europe alter Dante's death in 1321.

When Max Müller made his plea for a Sanskrit Renaissance in the 1880s, no Dante of youthful promise had as yet appeared in India, to advance a counterplea or protest in behalf of the vernaculars. And in view of all that had been said a century earlier about the perfection of Sanskrit by Müller's most illustrious predecessor in Sanskrit studies, the revered father of "British Orientalism," Sir William Jones (1746-1794), it had seemed to many

## Dante and the "Quest for Eloquence" 85

enthusiasts of the language that no Dante could conceivably appear. In an often-quoted paragraph of his Third Annual Discourse before the Asiatic Society of Bengal, delivered on February 2, 1786, William Jones had not hesitated to say that the Sanskrit language, as it had just come to be known, "is of a wonderful structure; more perfect than the *Greek*, more copious than the *Latin*, and more exquisitely refined than either." Yet that was but the first part of that epoch-making passage, in which Jones says further that Sanskrit bears to those Western classical languages

> a stronger affinity, both in the roots of verbs and in the forms of grammar, than could possibly have been produced by accident; so strong, indeed, that no philologer could examine them all three, without believing them to have sprung from some common source, which, perhaps, no longer exists: there is a similar reason, though not quite so forcible, for supposing that both the *Gothic* and the *Celtic*, though blended with a very different idiom, had the same origin with Sanskrit; and the old *Persian* might be added to the same family.[11]

That famous "philologer's passage" is unique in all the published works of Jones, including his letters. Never does he return to that briefly formulated judgment to develop its electrifying implications. Jones was by no means the first Westerner to study Sanskrit or to observe its affinities with the classical and modern languages of Europe. Yet it was clearly he who placed Sanskrit studies, and the consequent comparative linguistic studies, on a solid basis comparable to that of Western classical studies, through his organizing of the Asiatic Society in Calcutta (under the auspices of Warren Hastings, first Governor-General of British India) in 1784. Jones had arrived in India the year before, preceded by his international fame as a linguist. At Harrow and at Oxford, he had "outstripped his fellow-students, and apparently even his teachers, in Latin and Greek." During those same years, he had learned

French, Italian, Spanish, Portuguese, German, and Hebrew; and before departing for India, he had finally thrown himself "with special enthusiasm into the study of Arabic and Persian." Nevertheless it was as a lawyer and a judge, not a linguist, that he went to India; and to find time for Sanskrit studies there, he made it his habit, he said, to rise daily an hour before dawn. ([11] 1-5)

In 1785, his new friend, Charles Wilkins, "the first Englishman, and one of the first Europeans to study Sanskrit," had published his English version of the *Bhagavadgita*, "the first Sanskrit work to be rendered directly from Sanskrit into a European language." And immediately thereafter Jones began his own serious study of the language, though not without considerable difficulty at first, for competent Hindu teachers could not be easily induced to show him, much less help him to read, the closely-guarded texts. In the end, as Jones explains in a letter of September 17, 1785, it was not a high-caste Brahman, but "a pleasant old man of the medical cast" — a *vaidya* — who broke down, agreeing, in Jones's words, to teach "me all he knows about Grammar." A few months later, after he had gained the confidence of abler scholars, Jones wrote in another letter: "I am charmed with Sanskrit, in which I find tragedies and comedies at least 2000 years old; the good Brahmans, who do not know how much I am assisted by Latin and Greek, are astounded at my progress." ([11]5) Among the plays he first read at that time, one was no doubt the *Shakuntala*, his widely acclaimed translation of which appeared in 1789.

After Jones's death in 1794, the next major breakthrough in Sanskrit studies — and even more in vernacular studies — came with the founding of the College of Fort William in 1800, which was the work of Warren Hasting's most illustrious successor, the Marquess Wellesley. The language departments of that projected "Oxford of the East" had from the start been assigned the task, already undertaken for other motives by the Baptist preachers of the near-by Serampore Mission, to master all the languages of India and to "cut matrices and cast type"[12] so that in due course all the law and learning of the East might be printed and published in the oriental languages. With systematic translation of the Sanskrit texts into the Indian vernaculars as well as into English came the ultimate challenge to the high-caste Brahman custodians of the ancient purity of the language. And their inevitable surrender was clearly signaled at the annual "disputation" of the Fort William College language faculty presented with grand ceremony at the Calcutta residence of the British Governor-General on September 22, 1804.

The concluding speech of the "disputation" was to be delivered in Sanskrit by the most effective teacher at both the college and the Serampore Mission: the indefatigable William Carey, fisher of souls, first, but for thirty years also professor of Sanskrit and Bengali (and several other Indian vernaculars) at the College. In introducing Carey, the Marquess Wellesley delivered a speech that ended with these words: "Sanskrit learning, say the Brahmans, is like an extensive forest, abounding with a great variety of beautiful foliage, splendid blossoms and delicious fruits; but surrounded by a strong and thorny fence, which prevents those who are desirous of plucking its fruits, or flowers, from entering in. The learned Jones, Wilkins and others, broke down the opposing fence in several places; but by the College of Fort William, a highway has been made into the midst of the wood; and you, Sir, have entered thereby."[13] In his Sanskrit peroration on that day, Carey responded:

> My Lord, it is just that the language which has been first cultivated under your auspices should primarily be employed in gratefully acknowledging the benefit, and in speaking your praise. This ancient language, which refused to disclose itself to the former Governors of India, unlocks its treasures at your command, and enriches the world with the history, learning, and science

of a distant age . . . . What a singular exhibition has been this day presented to us! In presence of the supreme Governor of India, and of its most learned and illustrious characters, Asiatic and European, an assembly is convened, in which no word of our native tongue is spoken, but public discourse is maintained on interesting subjects in the languages of Asia. The colloquial Hindustani, the classic Persian, the commercial Bengali, the learned Arabic, and the primaeval Sanskrit are spoken fluently, after having been studied grammatically, by English youth. Did ever any university in Europe, or any literary institution in any other age or country, exhibit a scene so interesting as this?[14]

A year later, in 1805, the one remaining sanctuary of Sanskrit learning was finally penetrated. And it was the greatest by far of all the British orientalists, Henry T. Colebrooke, who then "gave the world," as H. G. Rawlinson has written, "the first account of the Vedas, hitherto jealously concealed by the pandits from European eyes." ([12] 546) After Colebrooke, came a host of French and German as well as English orientalists who worked tirelessly over all that had been recovered of the ancient Sanskrit legacy.

One is easily tempted, on superficial acquaintance, to view the labors of Wilkins, Jones, Carey, and Colebrooke as labors of the kind to which the Petrarchs and Erasmuses of Europe devoted themselves in trying to revive classical Latin. But in fact what we have in Jones and Colebrooke is quite the reverse of Petrarch's attitude. They were classical scholars in the modern, not the Renaissance sense of that term. Colebrooke's concern to encourage Sanskrit studies among the "native inhabitants of India" was quite like the concern of his peers in England, the Netherlands, and Germany at the time to encourage classical Greek and Latin studies at the great universities of the West. The very idea of such study was to prepare the mind of the present, more securely than it might otherwise be prepared, for a future very different from the past. To have provided the learned West with a *third* classical heritage to master, a heritage linking it to a common cultural ancestry with the peoples of distant India, was no small thing. But it was not for serious Englishmen — least of all for Englishmen in the employ of the East India Company — to work for a revival of India's Hindu past on the pattern of the dreams of Petrarch and Erasmus.

And as for William Carey and his fellow missionaries at Serampore, nothing could have been further from his intentions in studying Sanskrit than a revival of the civilization represented or mirrored in its classic writings. He studied Sanskrit so as to be able to draw on its lexical resources for his Bengali version of the Gospels. In a letter of that time of study, he observed to a friend that he had "read a considerable part of the *Mahabharata*, an epic poem written in a language most beautiful, and much on a par with Homer"; but, so far from wanting to revive the civilization represented in it, he went on to say that, unfortunately, the *Mahabharata* was not read in India as Homer is in the West, but rather as the "ground of faith to millions of the simple sons of men, and as such must be held in the utmost abhorrence." ([14] 73-74)

It is nevertheless true that, at the height of the excitement over the revelation of a pre-Islamic Golden Age of Hindu culture, there was at least a tendency among the British authorities to encourage a revival of the old-Sanskrit-based traditional systems of education. The assumption seemed to be that, by subsidizing such education, a new and yet traditional-minded elite of educators might be produced which would later assume the burden of providing basic education for the great mass of the population. But by the start of the 1820s, many native voices were raised in protest, charging that to give Hindu India, just recently emancipated from centuries of Muslim rule, back to the guidance of its old Sanskrit educators, would be like plunging the England of Shakespeare, Bacon, and Milton back into an age of schooling in medieval Latin. The leading voice of protest thus raised was that of Rammohun Roy (1772-1833), the learned Brahman who was later to be universally acclaimed "the father of Bengali prose"; and there can be no doubt, in retrospect, that he assumed an attitude toward the classical writings of India's Sanskrit Golden Age much more like that of Dante toward the Latin classics than like that of Petrarch or Erasmus.

Roy was one of the most cultivated men of his time. He wrote Bengali, Arabic, Persian, and later English, fluently. He was a master of Sanskrit, too; but it was not for him a living language. A Sanskrit-based system of education for modern India, he had protested, "could only be expected to load the minds of youth with grammatical niceties and metaphysical distinctions of little or no practical use to the possessor or to society. The pupils will there acquire what was known 2,000 years ago, with addition of vain and empty subtleties." A publicly-subsidized "Sanskrit system of education," he said, "would be the best calculated to keep this country in darkness, if such had been the policy of the British legislature."[15]

Thomas Babington Macaulay's notorious "Minute on Indian Education," dated February 2, 1835, owed much to Rammohun Roy. Largely on the strength of its arguments, the British authorities thereafter made English the language of secondary and higher education, leaving primary education to the regional vernaculars and the great hybrid *lingua franca* of mixed Hindi and Persian known as Hindustani — which was to be Gandhi's choice in the final debate to determine the national linguistic destiny of India after independence. "We must at present do our best," Macaulay had concluded,

> to form a class who may be interpreters between us and the millions whom we govern . . . . To that class we may leave it to refine the vernacular dialects of the country, to enrich those dialects with terms of science borrowed from the Western nomenclature, and to render them by degrees fit vehicles for conveying knowledge to the great

mass of the population.[16]

By adopting the Roy-Macaulay prescription for popular education in India, the British had quite deliberately favored what we might call the prospective Dantes of India's vernacular languages against her classizing equivalents of Petrarch or Erasmus. Support of Sanskrit studies, as also of Arabic and Persian studies, was not altogether abandoned however; and it was in fact the continued support of the British that made possible the work of Max Müller. Müller began his academic career as a professed disciple of Henry T. Colebrooke, though he was by no means a scholar of comparable abilities. He did some valuable work (marred, unfortunately, by evidence that he sometimes took credit for work done for him by others), particularly with his publication of a text and translation of the *Rig-Veda* with the commentary of Sayana (6 vols., Oxford, 1849-1874). Writing more as a publicist than a scholar he later said that his publication of that text, which has "never before been rendered accessible to the people at large," would produce, "nay, has already produced in India an effect similar to that which the first printing of the Bible produced on the mind of Europe." Müller spoke too of the importance for the West of this "first edition of the oldest book of the whole Aryan race," expressing confidence that, "as long as men value the history of their language, mythology, and religion, . . . this work will hold its place in the permanent library of mankind." ([12] 547)

Before Müller died in 1900, his academic peers had grown impatient with his penchant for exaggerating the importance of everything that occupied his attention. His manner had seemed serviceable for a time because it attracted popular attention and sometimes even public support for oriental studies. Yet in the end it had to be said that, "as a serious linguist," so John Gray summed it up in his Foundations of Language (1939), "he was scarcely successful, and his work in this field no longer merits consideration."[17] David Kopf takes the criticism a step further in *British Orientalism and the Bengal Renaissance* (1969). According to Professor Kopf, Müller's approach to the work of the earlier British orientalists sometimes involved a deliberate misrepresentation of their views. "It should be stressed," writes Kopf, "that the notion of a golden age of Indo-European peoples that commenced with Jones and was carried on by Colebrooke and Rammohun Roy differed considerably from the later nineteenth-century . . . myth of a Hindu golden age that Max Müller did so much to popularize, and that was influential in later Indian thought." Kopf speaks of Müller's "radical departure from the cultural beliefs" of both the orientalists and the disciples of Roy; he concludes, moreover, that "when in 1883 Müller gave his famous speech commemorating the fiftieth anniversary of Rammohun Roy's death, he was expressing a view of Indian renaissance totally alien to Rammohun's own tradition." ([13] 203-204)

And the same can be said of the divergence between Müller's views and those of William Carey and his scholarly associates at Serampore. As Professor Kopf observes, if Carey and his colleagues Joshua Marshman and William Ward had any sort of renaissance in mind for Bengal on the strength of their language studies and programs, it was "clearly not that of the classical humanist tradition." In their view, as against Müller's, "the key to European revitalization was not the revival of Latin or Greek . . . but the development of the popular languages of Europe." With the "integration of useful knowledge into the vernacular," the Serampore missionaries had concluded in a lengthy article on the subject, the emergent popular languages of Western Christendom "underwent a gradual improvement and obtained a firm foundation . . . through which the nations of Europe have since been impelled forever in a course of steady improvement." ([13] 156-158)

The valid parallel in Europe for what Jones, Colebrooke, Rammohun Roy, and Carey had undertaken to do linguistically for India is thus to be sought in Dante, with his *De Vulgari Eloquentia,* and not in Petrarch and his humanist successors, with their nostalgia for by-gone days of Roman glory and classical linguistic purity. And the parallel is being increasingly drawn by modern historians of linguistics as well as by students of the development of the vernacular literatures of India, especially Bengali, since the founding of the College of Fort William in 1800. In his *Short History of Linguistics* (1967), R. H. Robins, for instance, introduces the subject with a fine summary statement of Dante's objective as a practical linguist. "The serious study of the neo-Latin (Romance) languages," he writes,

> can be said to have been instituted by Dante's *De Vulgari Eloquentia* in the early fourteenth century, wherein he extolled the merits of spoken languages learned unconsciously in early childhood and contrasted them with written Latin consciously acquired as a second language at school through grammatical rules. In a celebrated passage Dante made a plea for the cultivation of a common Italian vernacular which should serve to unify the peninsula of Italy in the way that centralized royal courts did for other peoples."[18]

But then, drawing an explicit parallel between what Dante achieved for European linguistics at that early date and what Jones made possible for global linguistics in the nineteenth and twentieth centuries, Professor Robins notes first of all that Jones's exposition of the "historical kinship of Sanskrit, the classical language of India, with Latin, Greek, and the Germanic languages . . . came at a propitious time and to a Europe prepared for it." ([18] 134, 149)

It could be said, indeed, that by Jones's time the modern European nations "were just becoming aware of their own identity as separate from the strong Latin-Greek tradition" which had been cultivated for them not only by the old Renaissance humanists but, with an even sharper anti-historical emphasis, also by their neo-classical rationalists of the seventeenth and early eighteenth centuries.

In his attitude toward the evidences of common Indo-European linguistic origins which he traced through his study of Sanskrit, Sir William Jones was making a sharp break, according to Professor Robins, with the classical and neo-classical spirit of the immediately preceding centuries. The true Western prototype for such an attitude was plainly to be found in Dante. As Robins sums it up:

> Work on the historical relations of particular groups of languages by European writers may be said to have begun with Dante (1265-1321), though the relationship of Icelandic and English by virtue of resemblances in word forms had been asserted in the twelfth century by the brilliant 'First Grammarian.' Dante's *De Vulgari Eloquentia* has already been mentioned in connection with the post-medieval rise in status of the European vernacular languages; this same work gives an account of the genesis of dialect differences and thence of different languages from a single source language as the result of the passage of time and the geographical dispersion of speakers. Dante recognized three properly European language families: Germanic in the north, Latin in the south, and Greek [Byzantine] occupying part of Europe and adjacent Asia. He divided the contemporary Latin area into three distinct vernacular languages [whose] common descent was shown by the considerable numbers of words that each shared with the others and which could be referred to a single Latin word. ([18] 165)

On the subject of the common origin of the European languages, Dante goes into much greater detail than Jones does in his celebrated "philologer's passage." Most interesting in this respect is Dante's view that when the speakers of the parent language arrived on the borders of the West and then broke up into three branches, they were probably all new-comers entering Europe from the East for the first time; yet it is not impossible, he hastens to add, that some of them at any rate might have been Europeans to begin with, in which case, from an ethnic standpoint, their entry with the new language might actually have been

# Dante and the "Quest for Eloquence"

a re-entry or return. That bit of scholarly caution has a very modern ring about it. But even more modern is his economic-determinist account of the ultimate origin of the multiplicity of languages in the world.

In the *De Vulgari Eloquentia*, Nimrod the masterbuilder of Babel is very impressively represented for us as nothing less than a modern transnational industrial giant born long before his time. His expressed aim is to build a towering city of man that will dwarf all of nature. To that end he has recruited workers from every part of the world. Or, as Dante puts it, echoing the biblical tale: "Almost the whole human race had come together for this work of iniquity." But Nimrod has also developed a bold new industrial technique for maximizing productivity in the ancient building trades. It is a caste-like, rigidly-specialized "division of labor" the operation of which Dante thus describes, no doubt with the closed-shop caste tendencies of his own Florentine professional guilds and labor unions in mind:

> Some were giving orders, some acting as architects, some forming the walls, some making them straight with levels, some laying on mortar with trowels, some quarrying stone, some transporting it on land, some on the sea, and various other groups were engaged in various other occupations. ([1] 10)

How far the colossal transnational enterprise had progressed before the curse of confusion was called down upon it, Dante does not say. Yet what it amounted to finally was really no more than a confinement of each specialized group or caste to its inbred jargon; so that, as Dante says,

> all the architects had one language, all those rolling stones, one, all those preparing them, one; and so forth with each group of workers. And thus to the extent that there had been varieties of skills contributing to the labor, to that extent the human race was now divided into language groups; and to the extent that their skills were more noble, to that same extent their language was

more crude and barbaric. ([1] 11)

In other words, the division of labor introduced to intensify production was turned against itself; the unity of the enterprise was completely fragmented. And since Nimrod as master-builder was "one of a kind" in his own scheme, his fate was to end up babbling on and on in a tongue intelligible only to himself (a line of which Dante troubles himself to transcribe in *Inferno* XXXI, 67). Once he has traced the original caste-jargon from which all the European languages derive to the borders of the West — implying that all the other caste-jargons produced by the curse of Babel were making their way at about the same time to other parts of the inhabitable world, north, south, east, and west — Dante will note that while most of the subsequent linguistic diversification has been more or less natural, whenever something of the old arrogance takes possession of a group, there is apt to be a renewed hardening into jargon, working itself down to divisions and subdivisions of languages and dialects and sub-dialects almost *ad infinitum*.

Significantly, William Carey will find in his study of the actual speech of the people of Bengal in the early nineteenth century precisely the kind of hardening into exclusive jargons that Dante describes. Carey, it has been said, gave the idiomatic language of Bengali "merchants, fishermen, women, beggars, day-laborers, and other common folk" the dignity of "a minute and sympathetic observation" which they had never before received. In the process he had noted how each distinguishable group appeared to speak fluently enough within its own circle of intimates, but not in general discourse with "outsiders." In general discourse, he observed, they fall back on "a confined dialect composed of very few words which they work about and make them mean almost everything." ([13] 93, 92)

Yet it must be said that Dante's method of comparative study on all levels of language diffusion and diversification was far in advance of Carey's and indeed of the methods of most comparatists before the great school of Franz Bopp (1791-1867) began to shape itself in the late nineteenth century. What Dante contributed to subsequent methodology is thus aptly summed up by Professor Robins:

> As diagnostic marks of his language divisions Dante used a method seen again in J. J. Scaliger [1540-1609] and enshrined as a labeling device in the much later binary division of Indo-Europe into the *centum* and *satem* groups. He chose a single word meaning and noted its expression in different languages; thus the Germanic languages reply in the affirmative with "iò" (ja, etc.), and the three Latin-derived languages use "sì" (Latin *sic*) in Italy, "oc" (Latin *hoc*) in southern France, and "oïl" (Latin *hoc ille*) in nothern France.... From this division spring the names of the main linguistic divisions of France, *Langue d'oc* (Provençal) in the south and *Langue d'oïl* in the north. Within these language areas Dante was keenly aware of dialectical differences, and in subsequent chapters he gives a most detailed and well exemplified survey of the Italian dialects.... Alternative models of the historical relations of languages were not lacking during the period from Dante to Sir William Jones... it was just that they were not taken up and developed ([18] 165-166)

Jones's conceptual or theoretic contribution to the study of the historical relations of languages was really limited, as we have already suggested, to the principles implied rather than defined in that marvelously brief "philologer's passage" of 1786. Yet that passage served, of course, to open up a "veritable mine of precious stones in Sanskrit," as well as in Persian and other related Eastern languages, for the use of later European linguists. ([11] 30) The precious stones in Sanskrit proved to be invaluable because they had centuries before been prepared for comparative study by classical Indian linguistic scholarship, which is unquestionably much older than anything comparable in the West. Neither Greek nor Latin language studies can be said to have ever possessed what Professor Suniti Kumar Chatterji has called "that superb analysis and wealth of detail which have made Sanskrit grammar one of the foremost achievements of the human intellect." On the other hand, as Chatterji hastens to acknowledge, the "work of Indian grammarians was imperfect in this, that language was conceived by them to be a static phenomenon." ([11] 32) It was Jones who, by returning to the perspective of Dante (for whom change was the very essence of living language), made possible the reworking of India's traditional linguistics into a form compatible with the historical linguistics of the West. That linguistics, as Professor Robins stresses, had been given a remarkably solid foundation in the *De Vulgari Eloquentia*; yet, largely because of the nostalgic distractions of the Renaissance humanists, it must be said that, "from Dante onwards," till the time of Jones, the development of historical linguistics remained at best fragmentary and discontinuous. ([18] 149)

## 2. Bengali's Development on the Latin-Italian Model

Anyone who turns from Dante's discussion of the dialects of Italy and his evaluations of their literary potentials to study the record of what the chief linguists of the College of Fort William tried to do for India's regional vernaculars in the early nineteenth century will be struck at once by the parallels. And in the case of Bengali, especially, parallels are traceable straight down through the century from William Carey at its beginning to Rabindranath Tagore at its close. Both Carey and Tagore, significantly, have repeatedly been compared with Dante as language developers; and the comparisons, generally speaking, have been apt. For, while neither Carey nor Tagore ranks as a Dante linguistically or literarily, between them, as the beginning and end of a long line of development, they certainly did for Bengali something very like what Dante did for his native Tuscan.

We read in George Smith's *Life of William Carey* (1885), for instance, that, at Carey's touch, Bengali "arose from the tomb of Sanskrit as Italian did from Latin under Dante's inspiration" ([14] 202); while in his *Studies in Bengali Poetry* (1962) the eminent poet and critic Humayun Kabir — who was then India's Minister for Scientific Research and Cultural Affairs — did not hesitate to draw this highly suggestive comparison:

> Dante in Europe offers an example where the work of a single poet lifted the dialect of a province to the status of a world language. The achievement of Tagore is in some ways even more striking. Dante was born in the expansive days of the Italian renaissance. Italy was divided into a hundred principalities but stirred with a new consciousness of freedom . . . . Dante's genius shone the more brightly in the context of his surroundings. In the case of Tagore, the contribution of the environment was at times negative. His influence on the environment was in fact greater than that of the environment on him . . . . Renascent Bengal found in Tagore's work a message of liberation and a reflection of its own aspirations. [He] crystallized into forms of beauty the inchoate feelings and vague aspirations that were stirring in the Indian consciousness. Through their expression in his work, suppressed emotions found a new direction and urgency . . . . Tagore's intimate connection with the Indian National Congress from the day of its foundation was no accident. He brought the message of a new awakening to India just as Dante had done to a resurgent Italy.[19]

What strikes one forcibly in that extended comparison is the ease with which Professor Kabir passes from Dante the medieval poet writing in a provincial dialect, to Dante outshining the luminaries of the subsequent Renaissance, to Dante bringing to "resurgent Italy" the same message of a new awakening that Tagore brought to modern India. We have there not the real Dante, but a Dante projected forward as a living cultural force across the breadth of many centuries, down to the eve of Italian unification and independence in the 1860s and 1870s. Tagore was, of course, a contemporary of India's modern resurgence; a contemporary and friend, in fact, of the man who did for India within five and a half *years* of Tagore's death in 1941 what Mazzini, Cavour, and Garibaldi managed to do for Italy only five and a half *centuries* after Dante's death in 1321.

From a political standpoint it is certainly possible to draw a parallel between the Italian "risorgimento" that started building up from the mid-eighteenth century to culminate in Mazzini's "Young Italy" movement in the nineteenth, and the Indian resurgence that started with Rammohun Roy in the nineteenth century and culminated with Gandhi's "Young India" movement in the twentieth. But such a parallel obviously has nothing to do with Dante, who is even further removed chronologically from Mazzini than Kabir, the bhakti poet of the sixteenth century, is from Gandhi. The Tagore-Dante parallel is valid only in terms of the *preceding* linguistic-literary developments. What happened to Bengali during the nineteenth century at the hands of William Carey, Rammohun Roy, the prose-master Vidyasagar, the marvelously bilingual poet Michael Madhusadan Datta, and India's first great novelist Bankim Chandra Chatterji, by way of preparation for Tagore, certainly parallels what was done for "emergent" Italian by Dante's literary precursors of the thirteenth century. Dante, to be sure, was very conscious of what had been done for Italian before him. Indeed, as T. S. Eliot and Ezra Pound have pointedly observed, no one else in all of literary history has celebrated his precursors more ably than Dante. We find him again and again distinguishing their specific contributions to the development of the literary capacities of his language not only in his *De Vulgari Eloquentia* and his earlier *Vita Nuova* and *Convivio* but, even more, in the many passages of his *Commedia* which have long since established themselves as surpassingly beautiful components of a genuinely critical and soundly reasoned *ars poetica*.

Anyone attempting a *de vulgari eloquentia* for the Indian regional languages would of necessity have to begin with the work of William Carey at Serampore and at the College of Fort William. Carey's biographer George Smith notes that, in the very first official notice of the language "offerings" of the College, Carey himself had stressed that "all the Eastern languages are to be taught in it," not only *learned* Arabic, *classic* Persian, and *primaeval* Sanskrit, but also the principal languages actually spoken by the people. As George Smith then specifies: "The five great vernaculars of India" — Bengali, Maratha, Telugu, Tamil, and Kannada — "were accordingly named, and the greatest of all, Hindi, which was not scientifically elaborated till long after, was provided for under the mixed dialect or *lingua franca* known as Hindustani." ([14] 162)

That last apparently-cryptic phrase, about Hindi being "provided for under . . . Hindustani," refers to the fact that, from the beginning, language teaching at the College had been departmentalized not according to the essential characters of the languages as spoken but according to their scripts. This was done because the chief aim of the British authorities in introducing language instruction at the time had been not simply to teach new administrators of the East India Company to speak, read, and write in the oriental languages but, even more, to "promote the rise of printing and publishing" in those languages. Scripts, and the writing reforms required to standardize them for casting type-fonts, thus became the central concern. Before the coming of the Europeans with their Roman alphabet, the two basic types of script in use had been the native Indian and the Perso-Arabic. The native Indian types had become very numerous, varying from region to region, though all appeared to have a common ancestry — not, to be sure, in the now-familiar Sanskrit script, for Sanskrit had been written traditionally, if written at all, in whatever script happened to be used for the local vernacular. British insistence on a single script for standardized printing of Sanskrit texts produced the handsome Nagari now in use. Nagari had traditionally been the humble script of the "greatest of all the vernaculars," Hindi (and several other Hindu speeches); but, after the change brought upon it by the British, it soon "came to acquire," as Professor R. C. Majumdar puts it, "a new sobriquet, the *Deva-nagari* or 'the Divine Nagari,' because Sanskrit as the language of the Gods came largely to be printed in it."[20]

Because he had come to the College language faculty with full mastery of Bengali and Sanskrit, William Carey was made the head of the department specializing in Indian-script languages. Marathi, Telugu, Tamil, and Kannada, as well as Bengali and Sanskrit, came under his jurisdiction. By traditional right, Hindi with its Nagari script belonged there also. But since the primary concern was to print and publish, Carey quite intentionally let it slip out of his grasp. The argument was that, despite its traditional Nagari script, Hindi had let itself be absorbed almost completely in what had been originally only its hybrid offspring, Hindustani; and that, since that hybrid offpring had come to be written almost exclusively in Perso-Arabic, Hindi itself, as distinct from the hybrid, hardly existed at all in written form.

The historical pattern of development had been clear enough. Hindi, as the most widely used vernacular of India, had felt the strongest impact of the Persian speech of the Muslim conquerors. In the course of centuries, it had developed under Muslim rule quite in the way that Anglo-Saxon transformed itself, absorbing a tremendous body of French words, under Norman rule in England after 1066. In the form of Hindustani, in other words, it had early become a true *lingua franca* for communication between Hindus and Persian-speaking public officials everywhere in India; and, as a consequence, it came to be written more and more in the preferred script of those with whom communication was desired or most needed. In the eyes of those Persian-speaking officials (many of whom were high-caste Sanskrit speakers as well), the resultant speech they were often called upon to transcribe for illiterates could hardly be anything better than a camp-follower's mishmash, of utilitarian, but of no possible higher value. From that judgment of it came the name *Urdu*, which is a variant of the Turkish word for camp (cf. English *horde*).

At any rate, for having virtually abandoned its Nagari script, the greatest of the Hindu vernaculars came to be "provided for" not in William Carey's department but in the "Muslim dominated" Perso-Arabic-Hindustani department headed by Carey's arch academic "rival," John Gilchrist — a most extraordinary ex-doctor adventurer who came close to giving India, shortly after 1800, the very same national language that Gandhi tried so hard to give her down to the very hour of his death in 1948.

Carey and Gilchrist between them transformed India into what it has ever since remained: the largest linguistic-literary experimental laboratory in the world. They did, in diverse ways, exactly the kind of thing that Dante proposed should be done, in his *De Vulgari Eloquentia*, to develop a potential for eloquence in the vernaculars. Dante had called for open competition among the regional vernaculars of Italy, specifying, however, that he did not mean by that a blind preference for "one's own." "I, for one," he had hastened to assure his sophisticated reader by way of example,

> have the world as my native land, as the fish has the sea; and though I drank of the Arno before I had teeth, and though I have loved Florence so much that I have suffered exile unjustly for my love ... I have decided and firmly believe that there are many regions as well as cities both more noble and more delightful than Tuscany and Florence where I was born and am a citizen, and that there are many nations and peoples who use a language more delightful and more useful than the Latins. ([1] 9)

Yet Dante could hardly have permitted himself to play the Olympian in that fashion had he been, like Carey or Gilchrist, a language-department head in Calcutta. At the College of Fort William funds were typically scarce for subsidized research, faculty raises, and native teaching assistants, and competition was keen for students. Every year there were new challenges to be met, new programs to be formulated, claims to be pressed.

John Gilchrist, for instance, very early came up with a plan to raise Hindustani by bold experimental thrusts to the status of a major oriental literary language, on a par with what Anglo-Saxon became in England after the Normans finally gave up their old scheme to rule as Frenchmen over a united France and England. He asked that Hindustani not be judged by its present appearance, since, as he said in 1802, it is now "in fact still in its embryo stage." He had already undertaken what he called a "typographic reformation," of the written language, having devised ways, in both the Perso-Arabic and Nagari scripts, of "joining the letters of each vocable as much as possible." More important, he had already gone far in working out for every character of the Persian, Arabic, and Nagari alphabets a precise equivalent in the Roman alphabet. His long-range view was that, if Hindu and Muslim Indians could be induced to accept Romanization, Hindustani would at last become as much one in writing for both communities as it already was for both in speech. ([13] 82)

To get the language as actually spoken exactly right, Gilchrist made field trips to the regions where the purest use of it was made — Delhi, Lucknow, Cawnpore, Agra — and from all those places he "collected a band of men who were masters of the idiom," brought them back to Calcutta, and put them to work. With their help he produced, grammars dictionaries, and readers.[21] At one point he called for a British decision to drop Persian at once as the official language and substitute for it not English or Sanskrit but his hybrid Hindustani. Given adequate funding,

he then concluded:
> I shall engage soon to form such a body of useful and entertaining literature in that language as will ultimately raise it to that estimate among the natives which it would many years ago have attained among a more enlightened and energetic people . . . . May we not reason thus from analogy, that the Hindustani will ascend as high on the Indian scale . . . as the English has done in a similar predicament in our own country. ([13] 83)

Unfortunately for Hindustani — which is to say, for Gandhi's linguistically united India — John Gilchrist's tenure in the College of Fort William didn't last very long. After three years at his post, he found himself heavily in debt and lost his temper with the authorities. Months later, in 1804, he "boarded a ship for England," we are told, "and passed quietly from the Calcutta scene forever." ([13] 84) During the thirty years of Carey's tenure in the Indian-script languages department, specializing more and more in Bengali, the Hindustani Perso-Arabic department had five successive heads of relatively brief tenure, no one of whom was ever a match for Carey in academic in-fighting. Even after 1818, when British rule came to be extended over the whole of India, and it was obvious that Bengali could have very limited use for public administration outside the old Fort William Presidency, Carey would manage to keep his department well funded by persuading at least some of his superiors that the claims for Hindi-Hindustani, which he usually referred to as "that Mossulman dialect," were exaggerated. At one point he complained that, before his time,

> the Bengali language was almost wholly neglected by Europeans . . . from a supposition that the Hindustani (Urdu) is the language universally prevailing . . . . The mistaken idea that the Mossulman dialect of the Hindustani was the most prevalent language in India was probably the cause that formerly induced the greater number of those Europeans to study it in preference to

all others.

The harm of that, he added, was that the character of the hybrid made the Europeans despise all the vernaculars and therefore ignore the rest, including Bengali, the most beautiful — because the least Persianized and most Sanskritized — of them all. ([13] 164-165)

Like Gilchrist, Carey sought from the beginning to gather around him competent speakers of the living language. We noted before his observation that most Bengali speakers greatly limited the range of words they freely used outside the circles of greatest intimacy. To get at the fullness of the language as intimately spoken, he recommended to others his own practice of relying on children, for children "will catch up every idiom in a little time." His own children, he added, could "speak nearly as well as the natives, and know many things in Bengali which they do not know in English." ([14] 73) The *Dialogues* he compiled and composed, to which reference was made earlier, give an anthropologically accurate picture, now hardly available in any other source, of how the age-old divisions of Bengal society manifested themselves in the popular language, which was so characteristically distinctive for each segment or class of the social order. Like Dante's in the *De Vulgari Eloquentia*, Carey's aim was to enrich the local speech in two directions, which may be distinguished basically as horizontal and vertical. Horizontal enrichment was to be achieved, as we have been suggesting, by drawing on the specialized jargons of the trades and neighborhoods and family-kitchens to make them generally available to be used by all. ([13] 92)

But that was not enough for his purpose. As George Smith says of him, Carey had in mind very early to make a translation of the Bible that would do for the Bengalis nothing less than what "Jerome had first accomplished for the Latin Christians, Ulfila for our Scandinavian forefathers, Wiclif for the English, and Luther for the Germans." To be able to do that, he knew that he had to enrich the native speech with more than the varieties of common usage so accurately transcribed in his *Dialogues*. For the kind of enrichment he needed, he had to try to open up the local speech vertically; which is to say, he had to reach up into Sanskrit. "Without Sanskrit," writes Smith, "Carey found that he could neither master its Bengali offshoot nor enrich that vernacular with the words and combinations necessary for his translation of Scripture." ([14] 73)

Carey had in fact already brought out a Bengali version of the *New Testament* — with which he was far from satisfied — in 1801. But he set out immediately to equip himself to prepare a second edition in which the regional language would be brought much closer to Sanskrit. With the help of learned Brahmans, he set about to make Bengali the true heir of Sanskrit as he conceived Italian to be the heir of Latin. And it was then that he began his work of many years on his great *Dictionary of Bengali and English*, which began to appear in 1815 but was not completed until 1825, when, with its 80,000 words, it was published in three quarto volumes. The eminent Sanskrit scholar of a later time, H. H. Wilson, would say of it that "no language, not even in Europe, could show a work of such industry, erudition, and philological completeness at that time." Wilson declared that

> it must ever be regarded as a standard authority, especially because of its etymological references to the Sanskrit, which supplies more than three-fourths of the words; its full and correct vocabulary of local terms, with which the author's 'long domestication among the natives' had made him familiar, and his unique knowledge of natural history terms. ([14] 286)

Carey had very early begun to assert that "Bengali may be considered as more closely allied to Sanskrit than any other language of India," and he made it a boast that, not three-fourths, but "four-fifths of the words in the language are pure Sanskrit." ([20] 168) Indeed, in the various works that were written for him by his Brahman pandits at that time, it was later determined by actual count that as many as 88% of the words were pure Sanskrit. Fortunately, by that time, Sanskrit had come to be printed exclusively in the Nagari script it shared with Hindi; but, when it was written in the Bengali script, as it had traditionally been in Bengal, it was virtually impossible to detect much difference between it and what Carey's pandits were calling or passing off as "enriched Bengali." ([13] 113-114)

The worst of it was, as G. A. Grierson would later complain, that for almost every one of the Sanskrit terms introduced to enrich Bengali there had been ready at hand a "vocable of pure growth", that was integrally and organically a part of the vernacular. Grierson will make the point that, through such needless borrowing, Bengali was almost fatally "split into two sections — the language understood by the people, and the literary dialect, known only through the press and not intelligible to those who do not know Sanskrit," with the inevitable effect that "literature has thus been divorced from the great mass of the population." Even more harshly, and in a spirit closely akin to that of Dante in the *De Vulgari Eloquentia*, Grierson was to conclude that "Bengali, as a vernacular, has been stunted in its growth by this process of cramming with a class of food it is unable to assimilate."[22]

In his *Bengali Literature* (1948), looking back to the time of Carey, Professor J. C. Ghosh carried the criticism a step further, noting that the splitting of the language into two sections of opposite character — its artificially induced polarization into high and low extremes — often came to make its presence felt in one and the same author. Citing the case of Mrityunjay Vidyalankar, the most famous of Carey's pandits, Professor Ghosh writes: "Mrityunjay was an eminent Sanskrit scholar, but . . . as a writer he never struck his proper level, and his style is either too colloquial to be literary or, more often, too highly Sanskritized to be regarded as Bengali." ([15] 101) Such overpowering, inorganic, "enrichment", of a vernacular by excessive borrowing from the reigning grammatical language was precisely what Dante had warned against most sharply, singling out the Sardinian dialect of his day for special criticism in that regard. By making itself so dependent on Latin for its vocabulary, Dante had written, Sardinian had virtually surrendered its birth-right as a natural, living mother-tongue, and now hardly deserved to be called a language at all. "Incapable of creating a dialect of their own," he then concluded, anticipating the severity of Grierson's judgment of Bengali as developed by Carey's pandits, "the Sardinians imitate Latin as if they were not men but monkeys." ([1] 19)

Professor Ghosh will note that, when Bengali was finally freed from the hands of the excessive Sanskritizers gathered around Carey, efforts began in earnest to undo the damage, as far as possible, and once again enhance the processes of natural growth. In this linguistic reform, the Westernized writers starting with Rammohun Roy led the way. And the greatest credit in this regard, Ghosh will say, belongs to the most distinguished successor of Roy among the Westernizers, Iswar Chandra Sarma (1820-1891), who was awarded the title Vidyasagar shortly before his appointment as Head Pandit at the College of Fort William. Of that great Bengali educator, Ghosh writes:

> Vidyasagar brought to the service of his mother tongue the great acquirements of his classical scholarship.... Before him the language was uncouth and unshaped, and in confusion, but Vidyasagar gave it order and system, clear meaning and correct form.... The pandits of Fort William College, the British missionaries, and the other native and foreign writers before Vidyasagar, had overloaded their language with Sanskrit words and had added unnaturalness to unintelligibility by blindly following the syntax either of Sanskrit or of English. But Vidyasagar borrowed no more than could be harmoniously blended with Bengali and was necessary to strengthen and clarify its native genius.... The writers before him had observed an arbitrary divorce between

Chalit-bhasa (colloquial language) and Sadhu-bhasa (literary language), and their style had faltered between the coarseness of the first and the pedantic obscurity of the second. But Vidyasagar reformed them both and created a style which combined the naturalness of the one with the strength of the other.... Now a new harmony, "the other harmony of prose," was born in our language. ([15] 125-126)

All modern historians of Indian literature agree that the Sanskritization of Bengali had been carried to suffocating excess under Carey's influence, and that the reforms of Roy and Vidyasagar were absolutely necessary. Yet scholars concerned less with India's literary history than with her ethnic, religious, and political history are still apt to stress that Carey performed what they call a great national service, whether intentionally or not, by insisting on such Sanskritization. As Professor R. C. Majumdar notes, the books written in the style favored by Carey and his pandits were indeed

> intelligible only to a few, and are now generally forgotten. Nevertheless, their authors did a great service to the Bengali language by saving it from the dominating influence of Arabic and Persian which overtook Hindi. It is a remarkable fact that while the languages of Upper India came to be more and more Persianized and Arabicized, the Bengali language, since the beginning of the nineteenth century, deliberately cast off this foreign influence and looked for sustenance and development to the rich resources of Sanskrit. ([20] 168-169)

Majumdar's point is, of course, that, had the regional vernacular of Bengal not been so thoroughly de-Persianized and re-Sanskritized as it in fact was under Carey's influence, its renaissance might never have taken the form it actually did, which had the effect of inspiring Hindu writers in all other regions of India to de-Persianize and re-Sanskritize their regional vernaculars. Ironically, because it had been assigned not to Carey's but to Gilchrist's department at Fort William College, Hindi, despite the traditional Nagari script it would thereafter share with Sanskrit, could not initially benefit from the example of Bengali. Decades were to pass before a movement arose to de-Persianize and re-Sanskritize it to a comparable extent. And there is a double irony in the fact that the first time a course in Hindi written in Nagari was offered under British auspices in India, it was the Hindustani department at the College that offered it, with Carey in vehement opposition. Carey saw it as a "Mossulman ruse" to catch him and his department in a pincer movement. In his view, Hindi as spoken had been so thoroughly Persianized that, to write it in Nagari would amount to transliterating it from Perso-Arabic. And that was not very far from the attitude of those who proposed the course. Their idea, anticipating that of Gandhi a century later, was to advance the single hybrid speech, Hindustani, on a double track with two scripts, one preferred by the Indian Muslims and traditionally used by them, the other preferred by the Indian Hindus, though long neglected by them. The argument was that such a development of Hindustani in two scripts would quickly establish it as the all-India language of the future without creating an insuperable barrier between the Muslim and Hindu communities. ([13] 165,218)

But that idea ran exactly contrary to Carey's which had been to emancipate Bengali, first of all, and then the other chief Hindu languages, from the Muslim linguistic dominance that had reduced Hindi, in his view, to a "Mossulman dialect." He therefore accused the advocates of Hindustani in two scripts of trying, by that means, to reassert Muslim dominance on a linguistic level when such dominance was no longer possible on a political level. And his attitude was strongly supported by his native Hindu aides. The result was that the Hindustani department's scheme quickly backfired. Instead of outflanking Carey's Bengali with their two-pronged attack, they succeeded rather only in dividing their own ranks all to the advantage of Bengali; for, in time, the notion of writing Hindi in Nagari, after many generations of neglect, excited an unrestrainable Hindu-nationalist passion to de-Persianize the speech itself and re-Sanskritize it so that it too, not less than Bengali, might one day be able to "boast" of being 88% Sanskrit in its vocabulary.

Once he had set his Bengali on what he deemed to be the right course for it, Carey was content to see the British authorities displace Persian with English — not Hindustani or Sanskrit — as the all-India official language, thereby leaving the vernaculars to fend for themselves, as it were, on their own merits. Bengali, in his view, had already established itself as the premier literary language of modern India, as the legitimate heir to Sanskrit. He pointed to "original prose works on a wide range of topics by Bengali writers" in the 1820s, to tracts and treatises "debating contemporary philosophical and religious problems," to Bengali essays in social criticism, to newspapers, and he took pride in having paved the way for all of that. ([13] 218-219) He had, of course, every right to be proud; for, as the learned Bengali lexicographer Ramkamal Sen observed in 1830: "Whatever has been done towards the revival of the Bengali language, its improvement and in fact the establishment of it as a language, must be attributed to that excellent man, Dr. Carey, and his colleagues." ([15] 102)

For Bengali literature, "the growth of prose," writes Professor Ghosh, "was the main thing in the years 1800 to 1850." In its first appearances it was "clumsy and club-footed, pedantic and text-bookish, involved in syntax and loaded with jaw-breaking classical terms"; and it could hardly have been otherwise, Ghosh adds, since it was not in its beginnings "a spontaneous growth from the natural language of the people, but an artificial coinage of the pandit, who created it with the help of dictionary epithets from Sanskrit." ([15] 120) Rammohun Roy and Vidyasagar succeeded in redirecting that growth and thereby paved the way for Bankim Chandra Chatterji (1838-1894), "the greatest Bengali novelist and the founder of the modern school of Indian fiction," who quickly became and remained the most widely-read Indian author down through the first several decades of the twentieth century. ([15] 152)

Bengali poetry, during the early decades of the nineteenth century, got off to an even worse start than prose, writes Ghosh, being "as meagre in quantity as it was old-fashioned and inferior in quality." ([15] 119) The most famous Bengal poet of the period, Iswar Chandra Gupta (1812-1859), quickly eclipsed himself as a poet by becoming the leading journalist of his day. He is important historically because he was the first poet to leave the "beaten paths of devotionalism and eroticism" to write on matters of public interest, from the standpoint of an ardent nationalist and social reformer; but he "was too little an artist," Ghosh concludes, to ever become more than "a journalist in verse." Soon after Iswar Gupta, however, came Michael Madhusudan Datta (1824-1873), who did for Bengali poetry what Vidyasagar had done for Bengali prose. Madhusudan Datta, writes Professor Ghosh, "is the earliest, and the greatest, product of Western influence," and "undoubtedly the most interesting figure in our history." It could be said that he was first, by intention, an English poet — dreaming of achieving poetic fame in that language — and later "a Bengali poet almost by accident." Yet, precisely because he had immersed himself so completely in English poetry, he was able to substantiate the truth of his later boast that Bengali could do all that English could do, since it was indeed the "daughter of Sanskrit," and since "nothing was impossible for the child of such a mother" — not even poetically effective use of the blank verse of Shakespeare and Milton ([15] 134-142)

Vidyasagar, Bankim Chandra Chatterji, and Madhusudan Datta prepared the way for Tagore, the full flowering of the Bengal Renaissance, in whom the Italian promise of Bengali seemed at last to be fulfilled. The Nobel Prize awarded Tagore in 1913 for his Bengali poetry meant that the Western literary world had accepted Bengali as a world literary language. Tagore had not produced a *Divine Comedy*; yet there could be no mistaking the fact that, even with the English versions he had himself made of his lyrical poetry, he had achieved something comparable to the *dolce stil nuovo* — the sweet new style of Tuscan poetry — that had made Dante famous among his near and distant peers writing in the European vernaculars. In Professor Ghosh's words:

> Tagore's recognition in Europe was gained by the English *Gitanjali*, a volume mainly of devotional songs. But to his countrymen, and to those who can read him in the original, Tagore is first and last a writer of lyric poems and songs of love and nature, and that is how, they think, he will live the longest. His lyric impulse, which flowed early, showed no sign of abatement for over sixty years, from the passionate freshness of the early, "Awakening of the Fountain" to the thought-darkened "Last Songs" of a few years before his death. As a poet he has achieved more than average success in almost all the forms of his art, but he is greatest in the lyric, where his twin gifts of poetry and music blend most happily . . . . Poetry and music run into each other in his work as inseparably as form and color in natural objects, and it is difficult to say which of the two was his primary gift; though the probability in the present writer's opinion seems to be in favor of music. ([15] 183)

Here the parallel between the young Dante of the *dolce stil nuovo* and Rabindranath Tagore is perhaps strongest. By the time he wrote his *De Vulgari Eloquentia*, while his *Commedia* was still but a vision, Dante had persuaded himself that the literary form best suited for poetic eloquence in the vernacular was not the ballad or the sonnet, which were already popular, but the *canzone*, the true song. "Although everything we write in verse is a song," Dante had observed, "only *canzoni* happen to have this word in their name"; and that is so because they alone "in themselves accomplish all that they are supposed to do" musically, as sonnets and ballads and other related forms do not. Both melody and rhythm have to be added instrumentally to sonnets to complete the intended effect, and ballads, intrinsically more musical, still "have need of dancers to keep time, who thus bring out their forms." Only the true songs have it all in themselves, says Dante; that makes them "nobler than ballads, and consequently their metrical form should be considered the noblest of all, since no one may doubt that the ballad surpasses the sonnet in nobility." ([1] 37-38) Some modern scholars have tried to interpret Dante's text on this point so as to suggest that he is there claiming the maximum possible independence of the poetic song from music, on the romantic assumption that unheard melodies are sweeter than heard. But the eminent Dantist, Dino Bingongiari, in his authoritative notes on the text has put such interpretations to rest.[23]

Dante was not a master composer like Tagore. But the value he placed on the total fusion of heard music, real music, and words in the true poetic song is made plain in his *Commedia* itself where, upon entering the supersensory realm of *Purgatory*, it is the power of music that makes him cling for a final moment to sensory experience. The spirit of the great musician and singer of his age, Casella, is there asked by Dante to sing one of those love-filled songs that thrilled and overwhelmed his soul on earth. And Casella sings one of Dante's songs which he had "musicalized" for his friend, and, once again, all who hear it listen spellbound, forgetting where they are. (Purg. II, 76-133) "Tagore's best songs," Professor Ghosh writes, "are perhaps unique in their combination of beautiful poetry and beautiful music, although the full appreciation of their music is only possible for an Indian audience." ([15] 183)

Thus, on the level of excellence attained in the lyrical use of their regional vernacular languages, the parallel between Tagore and Dante suggested by Professor Kabir is certainly most apt. Yet the merest glance at the very different political circumstances under which the two poets wrote must suffice to discount any notion that comparable literary achievements ought to have produced comparable natlonal-literary consequences. During the century before Dante made his name as a vernacular poet, his Tuscany had not been under the rule of foreigners, as Tagore's Bengal had been all through the nineteenth century. On the other hand, Dante's native Florence in Tuscany had never been in any sense a political capital of Italy as Bengal's Calcutta had in fact been the *de jure* political capital of British India since 1833, and its *de facto* capital since 1818, and even earlier.

Was Bengal conquered or emancipated by the British rise to power in the second half of the eighteenth century? There is obviously a sense in which Muslim-ruled India was conquered and Hindu India emancipated; and, in that sense, Bengal, where British power was initially concentrated, experienced "Hindu emancipation" most directly and most fully. Previously, Bengal had been but an outlying province of the Mughal Empire which had its throbbing capital in distant Delhi. But, under the British, Bengal's chief town, built up from nothing by the British, soon began to rival and then to surpass old Delhi, in cultural as well as political importance. The changed situation could hardly have pleased the old dominant Muslims of Bengal or the high-caste Hindus who had accommodated themselves to Muslim rule. But it was otherwise, as Professor Kabir has observed, for the new breed of Bengal-Hindu intellectuals whose emergence paralleled the development of British power. British rule was foreign rule, to be sure; yet, as Professor Kabir writes:

> There were however circumstances which led a large section of the people to accept the position without protest. The possibility that Bengal might, for the first time in Indian history, win national leadership helped to

reconcile the people to British hegemony.

The Hindu middle classes were obviously the more easily persuaded to adapt themselves to the situation, even to the point of eagerly cooperating with the British "in the evolution of a new culture." The Muslims, on the contrary, "labored under a sense of injury and refused to cooperate with their conquerors," so that their middle classes were disintegrated and impoverished, whereas, when the Hindus "were offered an access to the culture of Europe, they were able to accept it without any sense of struggle or conflict." ([19] 51-56) The unprecedented cultural importance Bengal was thus able to acquire under British rule — after centuries of provincial obscurity — is thus pointedly summed up in the often-quoted words of Sir Jadu-nath Sarkar:

> If Periclean Athens was the school of Hellas, the eye of Greece, mother of the arts and eloquence, that was Bengal to the rest of India under British rule, but with a borrowed light which it had made its own with marvelous cunning. In this new Bengal originated every good and great thing of the modern world that passed on to the other provinces of India. From Bengal went forth the English-educated teachers and the Europe-inspired thought that helped to modernise Bihar and Orissa, Hindustan and Deccan. The new literary types, reform of the language, social reconstruction, political aspirations, religious movements and even changes in manners that originated in Bengal, passed like ripples from a central eddy, across provincial barriers, to the furthest corners of India.

On the literary level, Bengali had indeed been the "quickest and most wholehearted in responding to the stimulus of the West," as Professor Ghosh says, so that it quickly "acquired the position of premier literature" among the vernaculars, and came to rank "next to English" — whose influences it so strongly reflected — as "the greatest modernizing force in contemporary India." ([6] 390-391)

Yet the question has to be asked: Could Bengali have done all that if it had been just one vernacular among many, like Dante's Tuscan, without the advantages of a "borrowed light" made available to it by a powerful imperial government? It is hardly an academic question since, in 1912, the year before Tagore won the Nobel Prize, the British authorities in Bengal shocked the local intelligentsia by starting to implement their secretly-made decision of the year before to move their imperial capital. It was to be relocated, in fact, 900 miles inland from Calcutta, in old Delhi, in the heart of the vast north central plain of Hindustan, where the local vernacular was not Carey's Bengali, which Tagore had now raised to world importance, but Gilchrist's hybrid Hindustani (already internally polarized as Hindi and Urdu), which was about to be taken up by Gandhi regardless of its Cinderella-status as a modern literary language.

That the move, announced as a *fait accompli*, or at least as a decision from which there could be no turning back, was a terrible blow to the Bengali intellectuals is beyond question. Sir Percival Spear refers to the decision to make it as "one of the few secrets successfully kept in modern India." It had been taken shortly after Lord Hardinge succeeded Lord Minto as Viceroy of India in 1910. The new Viceroy, writes Spear, surprised his critics by carrying through "with unflinching firmness against much local opposition in Calcutta the transfer of the imperial capital to Delhi." The old imperial policy traceable forward from Wellesley too Lord Curzon, the policy of benevolent imperialism that favored provincial Bengal over the ancient center of Indian power, was clearly about to end. Thus, as Spear puts it: "Calcutta and Lord Curzon at home were thunderstruck: neither forgot or forgave."[24] Yet the arguments for a move "up-country" were strong and had been strongly felt before Lord Hardinge's time. The difficulty in the past, Spear concludes, had always been to find a place whose historical associations might unite with practical convenience in justifying the large outlay which would be necessary. Delhi, covered by the Punjab and Frontier Province, possessing Mughal associations without important Mughal survivals, forming a vital center of communications and being near to Simla hills, now provided such a center. The decision was justified in the circumstances of the day, and it proved even more important than its authors imagined. It provided the monument in stone which the British had hitherto lacked, and the new India with a ready made capital. ([24] 334)

Thus, Tagore's Nobel Prize of 1913 for poetry in Bengali had come just after Calcutta and Bengal had abruptly been deprived of an advantage they had enjoyed for over a century. Would the move to Delhi deprive Bengali of the literary primacy that its great authors from Roy to Tagore, and especially Tagore, had earned for it under British rule? From a Western literary standpoint, at any rate, there was every reason to believe that it would not. In histories of Indian literature written in the West during the years that the monumental New Delhi was being built beside the old — the new capital was not officially inaugurated until 1931 — Tagore was rather consistently celebrated as having done for Bengali what Dante did for Tuscan, and, as Professor Kabir suggested, perhaps more. The treatment accorded him in Herbert H. Gowen's *History of Indian Literature From Vedic Times to the Present Day* (1931) was typical. Although more than three-quarters of the volume were devoted to Sanskrit literature before the Muslim invasions, the first words of its introduction were "Rabindranath Tagore," identified as the poet who, in modern India, most "worthily maintains the spirit of the ancient *rishis* — authors of the Vedic hymns — and who is "himself a happy proof of the essential continuity of Indian literature."[25] Later in the book Professor Gowen will not hesitate to say that "there is nothing greater in Indian literature than Tagore from the time of Kalidasa" and that "even Kalidasa does not illustrate the versatility or profundity of the modern muse" with that oversoul of his "doctrine of *jibandebata* . . . which binds in sequence the poet's successive incarnations and phases of activity." In the last paragraphs of the book, after noting that events "are moving rapidly towards a more consciously nationalized and unified India," the author concluded that in those events can "be felt the prophecy of a truly unified literature which shall have its Kalidasas and Tagores in abundance in the days to come." ([25] 570-571)

In Atulchandra Gupta's *Studies in the Bengal Renaissance* (1958), too, Tagore is treated as an authentic continuator of the tradition of the *rishis* and Kalidasa, as indeed a writer who has actually recapitulated in himself every important phase of India's long cultural and spiritual history. Sashi Bhushan Das Gupta in fact says of him in that volume that, while from a biographical standpoint he "represents practically a century of Bengali poetry" in himself, one needs to add also that, "from the historical point of view," he appears rather to be "the last important representative of Indian thought and culture."[26]

Needless to say, no historian of Italian literature or Latin literature could presume to couple the names of Dante and Virgil the way Professor Gowen coupled those of Tagore and Kalidasa in his prophecy about India's unified national literature of the future. Petrarch and the European Renaissance humanists who sought literary fame in a revived classical Latin might provide a late chapter or appendix for a history of Latin literature, but not Dante. Dante is clearly not a "last important representative" of anything, in the sense that such a designation could apply to Tagore. The author of the *Vita Nuova* plainly saw himself as a beginner. He knew he was creating a new language and a new literature that was altogether different from classical Latin, and different primarily in its popular Christian inspiration. Dante will say in the *Commedia* that what ultimately moved him to write his great poem in the vernacular was a kind of love that was unknown to the masters of ancient poetry, a love that would take him to heights where Virgil and Homer, for all their art and high Apollonian and Dionysian inspiration, could not presume to venture. For such poetry, he says, the development of the European vernaculars had been from the beginning preparing the way, with their poets who sang only of love, and of the chivalric courage and virtue that must attend true love in Christendom.

What Dante therefore traces in his *De Vulgari Eloquentia* is not a continuation of the Latin tradition down through the Middle Ages to his time, in expectation of a renaissance of the same kind of poetry that Virgil had written. What he traces is the preparation of a new literary medium capable of giving poetic expression to feelings unknown to the ancients but thoroughly well known to all the peoples of Christendom regardless of class or education. The learned of Christendom, he says, have clung too long to the language inherited from the pagan Romans, which is still indeed suitable for an administrating priesthood and an imperial bureaucracy. But, in the sphere of literature, there must be an end to desperate clinging to Latin. The popular languages of Christendom must be cultivated, refined, stripped of their purely local idiosyncrasies, while retaining their natural characters as mother-tongues. Dante's practical concern is with the dialects of his own Italy; and fortunately, he says, during the century before him, from Sicily to the Alps, a new class of writers skilled in Latin yet eager to write poetry in the regional dialects had begun to form itself. Though they used their native dialects, these new poets took care to universalize them as much as possible so that their peers in other parts of Italy would be able to read what they published, and perhaps respond in kind.

By 1300, the process of refining the regional dialects of Italy had brought many of those dialects to a degree of perfection that made them obvious competitors for literary primacy and, among the better poets in the regional urban centers, there was an open rejoicing in the competition. It is primarily to such poets that Dante addresses his treatise on eloquence in the vernacular. Anticipating by many centuries what John Gilchrist will propose for the development of Hindustani and William Carey for the development of Bengali, Dante urges that all the dialects be opened up for deliberate enrichment both horizontally, drawing on the resources of neighboring dialects and sub-dialects, and vertically, drawing on the grammatically-developed varieties of Latin, as well as on the more advanced vernaculars of Gallic Provençal and French. Let there be no restrictions, he says, on borrowing words and usages and techniques of verse from any source, ancient or contemporary, Italian or foreign; let there be full encouragement of the imitation of excellence wherever excellence is to be found; but in the end, let the arresting achievement of literary genius in the finished work of art be decisive.

In the actual competition, even with its sweet new style that had made its chief poets famous, Dante's Tuscan vernacular had to come from behind to win. Among the more formidable competitors from the beginning had been the cultured dialect of Sicily. By Dante's time, the grand island that had loomed so large in ancient Greek history had undergone a political fate much like that of India since the time of Alexander the Great. Long before India was conquered by them, armies of Islam had conquered most of Sicily; and their dominion there had lasted several centuries, till Normans of the same breed that conquered England in 1066 fell upon southern Italy and Sicily to emancipate the Italian natives, even as descendents of England's Norman conquerors would later emancipate India's Hindu natives from Muslim rule.

Arabic, Byzantine Greek, and French linguistic influences were strong in Sicily under the Normans; but they came to be felt as literary influences only after the Norman

Court in Palermo passed, by marriage, not force, under the control of the Swabian Hohenstaufen emperors, who were no more Sicilian or Italian than the Governors-General and Viceroys of British India were Indians. Under the Hohenstaufens, who had Dante's loyal support till their line expired, Palermo became for Sicily what Calcutta became for Bengal after the founding of the College of Fort William in 1800. Linguistic-literary experimentation found a most extraordinary patron in Frederick II (1194-1250). To carry on the bureaucratic business of empire, he was content to use clerical Latin, even as the Mughals and British used their Persian and English in India. The support he gave to poetry in the vernaculars was thus anything but imperial, or even national, in ultimate intent; it was an encouragement of poetry for its own sake, for its free-flowing, "Sunday-afternoon" vernacular vitality. In his *Languages of Italy*, Professor Giacomo Devoto very aptly sums up the contribution of the Hohenstaufens to the development of modern Italian during the period of its birth-pangs; and the terms he uses invite comparison and contrast with much that has already been said about British influence on the development of the Indian vernaculars in the early nineteenth century. The "basic quality" of the Swabian court in those early days, writes Devoto,

> is its open-door policy toward poets and the most diverse cultural currents — from France, from Provence, and from southern Italy as well as from Sicily itself. In contrast to the variety of dialects available and the Latin revival inherent in the rhetorical studies of the eleventh century, the court of Frederick II offers for the first time a suitable environment, capable of resisting both the prestige of Latin and the fragmentary quality of the local linguistic traditions. It elevates these local forms of speech to a literary level, at the same time rescuing them from traditional geographic limitations. The prestige that the vernacular derives from this process was no longer measurable according to the vertical dimension of tradition and time, but according to the horizontal

dimension of space. ([10] 207-208)

The Sicilian vernacular in those days enjoyed the same advantage that Bengali enjoyed while Calcutta remained the capital of British India. Dante dwells on the advantage in his *De Vulgari Eloquentia*. It was the court of German emperors, he says, that gave the Sicilians their early cultural reputation. While the Hohenstaufens reigned, and especially Frederick II and his noble son Manfred, Sicily enjoyed a reflected light, since "those of noble heart and endowed with gifts of divine grace strove to attach themselves to the majesty of these great princes"; the result was, Dante continues, that in the time of the Hohenstaufens everything good that came to Italy seemed to come by way of Sicily (even as in the nineteenth century, as Jadu-nath Sarkar will later say, "every good and great thing of the modern world" that came to India passed first through Bengal). "Every product of the efforts of the noblest Latin spirits" from all over Italy, Dante explains, sooner or later made its way to the Hohenstaufen throne room. And because that was located in Sicily, he concludes, "it happens that whatever writings our predecessors published in the vernacular were called Sicilian; we still hold to this practice, and it is unlikely that our posterity will change it." ([1] 19-20)

But the might of the Hohenstaufens failed. And what light their court had shed upon the native Sicilian literary culture failed with it. The noble spirits that had gathered around them in Sicily were scattered once more. Thereafter, at least from a political standpoint, the regional vernaculars of Italy were left to compete as equals. Among the chief competitors as the thirteenth century advanced was Umbria, land of Saints, with its devotional poetry, anticipating that of the Bhakti movement of sixteenth century India, with the great Kabir, so like Umbria's St. Francis, at its head. Economically-prosperous Lombardy, too, produced its share of competent poets in the vernacular, under strong French and Provençal influence.

Though it kept itself isolated from Italian affairs, Venice was always a potential contender, for its characteristic dialect had both the good taste and the mighty fleets of the Doges to support it. Yet, in Dante's view, the dialect that outstripped all of these, right down to his own time, was that of Bologna, the city that had become the center of legal study for all of Christendom. Dante praises the poets of Bologna for having opened their dialect horizontally, tempering their native speech with "elements adopted from either side," by the "combining of what I have called opposites," characteristic of neighboring dialects. ([1] 25-26 )

Still, before the vernacular competition entered its final phase, the best poets of Bologna itself had already turned elsewhere — that is, toward Florence, once Dante's own poetic genius had begun to make itself felt in the Tuscan vernacular. In his youth, Dante and his local peers, all of whom had learned so much directly or indirectly from Provence, and particularly from that *miglior fabbro del parlar materno* (that master-craftsman of the mother tongue) (*Purg.* XXVI, 117) Arnaud Daniel, had already broken the provincial crust of their local speech, while at the same time resisting the ever-powerful temptation to Latinize excessively. Then, as he more and more deliberately perfected himself in his art, Dante produced works in which even the most characteristically local touches acquired a seemingly unintentional universality. With that, his language raised itself at once to acknowledged literary primacy up and down the peninsula, leaving few literate Italians to doubt that, on the strength of literary merit alone, it would one day be adopted as the national language of all Italians.

When Dante died in 1321, however, Italy's national unification was, as we have already reminded ourselves, a long way off — as was the consequent adoption of a national language to be centrally enforced as such by political means. Who can presume to say how Dante's Tuscan would have fared if the city of Rome had become the capital of a united Italy immediately after Dante's death instead of five and a half centuries later? In his *De Vulgari Eloquentia,* Dante makes it rather plain that, from a linguistic standpoint, at any rate, he was by no means eager for the city of Rome to become for Italy what Paris had become for medieval France and London for medieval England. In fact, he speaks contemptuously of the Romans of his time who, he says, seemed to think they could lord it over the rest of the Italians simply because of their inherited name, even though, with their degenerate manners and foul-smelling personal habits, they were really anything but Roman in the old sense. He declares their speech to be "the ugliest of all the vernaculars," unworthy of even a moment's consideration in the search for vernacular eloquence. ([1] 17-18) If the ancient capital of imperial Rome had become the national capital of a united Italy in 1327, let us say, instead of in 1870, it would surely have meant that its dialect, or perhaps for a time even the revived classical Latin of Petrarch, would quickly have been declared the official national language (like Hindi in the 1950 Constitution of India) — despite the "provincial", protests of a Dante.

For two of the five and a half centuries that elapsed between Dante's time and the national unification of Italy with Rome as its capital, the Italians were indeed "gloriously divided," as Professor Kabir stressed in contrasting Tagore's social and political circumstances with Dante's. Despite the anti-vernacular bias of the leading humanists, the best writers of Italy in those "Renaissance" centuries were eager to make Dante's language their own, using it to produce masterworks that now rank just after Dante's *Commedia* in the canon of Italy's greatest writing. Among these one must include Petrarch's sonnets and songs, Boccaccio's *Decameron,* Ariosto's *Orlando Furioso,* and Machiavelli's *Mandragola* and *Prince.* Then, dating roughly from Machiavelli's death in 1527, came three centuries and more of division during which the Italians — like the Hindus of India for a much longer period — were anything but free.

Living under the heels of foreigners whose disdain for them was often insupportable, many talented Italians sought an escape abroad — as many Indians were to do between the time of Rammohun Roy and Gandhi; or if they remained at home, it was to nurse inchoate feelings of discontent, for which an outlet short of action was often sought by writing in the language and genres perfected by Dante, Petrarch, Boccaccio, Ariosto, and Machiavelli. Thus through all those centuries a great body of literature, some free, some servile, was produced in what had originally been the Tuscan vernacular of Dante. No literate Italian after Machiavelli's time ever doubted that, if Italy were ever free and united, the language of the *Commedia* and of the *Prince* would be its national language. Yet one must not imagine that it had established itself as the spoken language of a majority of the Italian people, much less as a language they could read or write.

On the contrary, as Professor Devoto observes, unlike the other major European literary languages, that of Italy "receives precocious stability precisely because it is addressed to a closed circle of men of letters." One could say that it became virtually what the humanists would have wished their revived Latin to become, or, centuries later in India, a revived classical Sanskrit. At any rate, "up to the middle of the nineteenth century," Devoto continues, "the Italian literary language had not been the language of a nation, but rather that of a caste of "letterati" or an "oligarchy." Even after the last remaining foreign rulers had been forced to "quit Italy" in the 1860s, from a linguistic standpoint the situation remained static. The underlying historical reality one needs to stress here, Devoto concludes, is that,

> ... unlike French and English, which became established because they were solidly anchored in the language used

in the royal chanceries, and unlike German, which, on the basis of the translation of the Bible by Martin Luther, penetrated into the consciousness of churchgoers, the Italian tradition is born as, and for centuries will remain, the language of an oligarchic minority . . . . The fundamental statistical fact, elaborated by T. De Mauro [and other competent modern scholars], proves that at the moment of political unification, the Italian literary language was a matter of concern to only 3% of the population, while 97% lived exclusively in the world of the dialects, which constituted real linguistic ghettos. ([10] 231,317)

Indeed, not until the middle of the twentieth century, after two world wars, with a long interval of rigorously centralized corporate-state rule sandwiched in between, had Italians been sufficiently moved about, from Sicily to the Alps, to make the national literary language, still essentially Dante's, the concern of all.

## 3. Ghandi and the Linguistic Surveys of Dante, Grierson, and S. K. Chatterji

In India, the six centuries and more that were given to Dante's Tuscan to affirm itself in free competition as the national language of the Italian people were eclipsed by the appearance of Mohandas Karamchand Gandhi (1869-1948) on the political scene just a few years after Tagore was a warded the Nobel Prize for his Bengali poetry in 1913. By a virtually general consensus of its chief historians, the year in which Gandhi assumed the political leadership in his country, 1919, has been called India's *Annus Mirabilis*. Yet for a sense of the tremendous eclipse of time that sudden emergence of the Mahatma represented for all in India who witnessed it, one must turn not to historical or journalistic accounts, however objective, but to the pages of Tagore himself. If Tagore was in any sense India's Dante, as Professor Kabir has suggested, it must be added at once that he was the first to recognize that Gandhi, with his *Young India*, weekly newspaper, which he began to edit in 1919, was its Mazzini; and that events, as a consequence, were about to be greatly rushed, leaving little time for literary elites to establish themselves as nationally-acceptable judges of what ought to be India's linguistic- literary future.

"No two persons," Jawaharlal Nehru had written of Tagore and Gandhi in 1946, "could be so different from one another in their make-up and temperaments." Tagore, Nehru stressed, was "the great humanist of India" as well as its towering poet. "Not Bengali only, the language in which he wrote," we read further, "but all the modern languages have been molded by his writings." Always the "aristocratic artist" — despite his "proletarian sympathies" — Tagore "represented essentially the cultural tradition of India, the tradition of accepting life in the fullness thereof and going through it with song and dance." Gandhi, on the contrary, was anything but a humanist or aristocrat in the cultural sense; to all who were present when he first appeared, he "seemed to emerge from the millions of India, speaking their language," and he represented, rather, in Nehru's words, "the other ancient tradition of India, that of renunciation and asceticism," even though his life was destined to be one "of concentrated and ceaseless activity." ([8] 342,361)

Tagore had said as much himself back in 1921. He had been perhaps the very first to hail Gandhi as the "Mahatma," as the "great-souled" leader who, simply by appearing on the scene, had instantly dwarfed everyone who had before him presumed to speak for India. It is true that the message of a "new awakening" for India had been echoing and re-echoing across the land for a century before the Mahatma's appearance. Bankim Chandra Chatterji had already stirred the emergent nation's soul with his *Vande Mataram* and Tagore himself had added his *Bharat Vidhata*, which is now the National Anthem. Yet never, during the century of intellectual accommodation to British rule, had the call to nationhood been more than a message of mere words. "Previously," wrote Tagore, anticipating the judgment of Jadu-nath Sarkar, "the vision of our political leaders had never reached beyond the English-knowing classes, because the country meant for them only that bookish aspect of it which is to be found in the pages of the Englishman's history."[27]

As an English-educated aristocrat, born into one of Bengal's proudest westernizing Brahman families, Tagore was never reluctant to acknowledge India's great debt to "English education." Even so, he dismissed the "vision of India" that it had inspired in even the best of India's new intellectuals as something altogether unreal. "Such a country," he said, "was merely a mirage born of vaporings in the English language, in which flitted about thin shades of Burke and Gladstone, Mazzini and Garibaldi. Nothing resembling self-sacrifice and true feeling for their countrymen was visible." Often during the decades of India's so-called Renaissance those who talked most eloquently of national ideals, Tagore said further, were the "most conservative in their social practices." Indian "brotherhood" was on their lips; but rarely did any of them so much as dream of an actual end to the "physical repulsion, one for the other, that we have between the castes." And then suddenly it happened. "At that juncture," writes Tagore, fully conscious of a spiritual eclipse of centuries of normal time,

> Mahatma Gandhi came and stood at the cottage door of the destitute millions, clad as one of themselves, and talking to them in their own language. Here was the truth at last, not a mere quotation out of a book. So the name of Mahatma, which was given to him, is his true name. Who else has felt so many men of India to be of his own flesh and blood? At the touch of truth the pent-up forces of the soul are set free. As soon as true love stood at India's door, it flew open; all hesitation and holding back

vanished. Truth awakened truth . . . . The thing that has happened is nothing less than the birth of freedom . . . the gain by the country of itself. ([27] 222-223)

Gandhi, with his daring cry of love, had summoned every man, woman, and child of India into a brotherhood of equality in freedom which was as necessary and as new to India as anything else that English education could conceivably have provided even if continued for half a dozen centuries more on the old terms. Gandhi simply eclipsed those centuries. The India of Rabindranath Tagore was not to have to wait as long as Dante's Italy for its nation-builders. Gandhi had not schooled himself in English ways in vain. Through many decades of his youth and manhood he had longed to hear Britain's imperial leaders say to him and to all Indians what Shakespeare's great Norman-English king is made to say at Agincourt, proclaiming blood brotherhood with even the meanest of his Saxon soldiers who would in that day's battle willingly shed his blood with him. What the British in India had failed to do, because they had not known or wished to know the Indian character well enough, the half-naked Mahatma had now done in their stead, proclaiming with a single love-filled cry (a cry matching Shakespeare's "be he ne'er so vile") that from that day forward there would be an end to caste-untouchability in India.

It was Gandhi who renamed India's untouchables the "People of God" (*Harijan*), which became the name of his indispensable weekly newspaper, previously called *Young India*, after Mazzini's "Young Italy" movement. "Forget altogether," he would later say, "that some are high and some are low. Forget altogether that some are touchables and some are untouchables . . . . This untouchability is the greatest blot on Hinduism, and I have not hesitated to say that if untouchability lives, Hinduism dies."[28] To draw all of India's Hindus into a truly integrated Hindu *community* — such as nobody before him had ever seriously deemed possible or right — was one of Gandhi's two great national crusades. The other, far more difficult, had as its avowed aim the integration of India's Hindus and her Muslims as citizens by birth of a common country in the modern national sense.

It is important to distinguish the three ideals of political integration that Gandhi pursued in the course of his long public career, because each has a special bearing on India's linguistic literary future. There was first the British ideal of "imperial integration." For a long time Gandhi was quite obviously ready to "join the empire" as an Indian ruling-class member. As Chandan D. S. Devanesen puts it in *The Making of the Mahatma* (1969), Gandhi had suffered in South Africa for three decades before he finally lost his faith in British Imperialism . . . . The student who studies the image of the British Empire Gandhi cherished until the aggravations in South Africa became unbearable, may conclude that a potential imperial statesman was lost in Gandhi. There was probably no non-European British subject anywhere in the Empire who strove harder than Gandhi to uphold what he described as "true imperialism."[29] He was bitterly disappointed, as he often said, to learn that the British were not "true imperialists" in what might be called the old Roman cosmopolitan sense, that they were nationalists in a racist sense who would rather quit India than accept men like himself as imperial "equals" in fitness to rule. Gandhi had agreed, in the early days, that "English should be the common language of the Empire" and that it should continue to be the all-India language even under self-rule within the Empire. But the painfully drawn out South African experience so "poisoned Gandhi's mind against the Empire," Devanesen concludes, "that even the good fruits of British rule in India lost their sweetness and became distasteful." Once he had reversed course, it was his absolute conviction that, if India was ever to rule itself, it would have to regard the best that English education had to offer as far more damaging to its character than the very worst it could conceivably suffer through

British economic exploitation or racial discrimination. That explains his later total rejection of any educational use of English in his projected India. ([29] 351)

Yet, could it not be said that, before their fall, India's Muslim rulers with their millions of converts had treated Hindu Indians even more disdainfully than the British? Gandhi rejected such a judgment. He felt that, except for the social exclusivity of the Hindu caste system, there would long since have taken place a true fusion of Indian Hindus and Indian Muslims. The Hindu untouchables had understood this, even though the sense of caste was "written in their hearts," so to speak. Many of them willingly entered the brotherhood of Islam when the opportunity offered itself. But, as there was no marrying or eating together for Muslims and Hindus on any social level, the outcast converts found themselves doubly rejected, not to say despised, by the great mass of their Indian brothers — for what they had become as much as for what they had been.

Yet, according to Gandhi, there was visible proof in present-day India that Muslim-Hindu fusion had always been possible, and that it had gone as far as the caste-exclusivity of Brahman Hindu India would allow. That proof Gandhi saw in the development of the hybrid Hindustani speech, which had resulted from the shared needs of Hindus and Muslims. Gandhi's attitude toward Hindustani was virtually identical with John Gilchrist's. And if one can trace a direct line in the development of Bengali from Carey to Tagore, surely a line quite as direct can be drawn from Gilchrist and his many successors to Gandhi in the case of Hindustani. Of course, there is one all-important difference. In the case of Hindustani, it must be said that, while the speech as speech showed a continuous vitality through the century, serving as the shared *lingua franca* for hundreds of millions of illiterate Indians, in its written forms it had become so polarized by the time Gandhi took up its defense that it proved easier in the end to partition India on the basis of script (following the example of the language faculty at Fort William College) than to keep it united on the basis of the spoken word.

In Gandhi's mind, the crusades against untouchability in the Hindu community and for a Hindu-Muslim national fusion were inextricably linked; and Hindustani was the key to both, since most of the converts to Islam, as has already been suggested, were probably untouchables. What could Indians as a whole — Hindus of every social level as well as Muslims — do together to manifest their national oneness, or to make themselves nationally one? That was always the question of highest priority for Gandhi the nation-builder. Indians had characteristically responded to common calls in the past by making them the occasion for further deepening of their ancient social, regional, ethnic, religious, and linguistic divisions. That was why, in Gandhi's view (by no means original with him), the Indian people had always been so easily defeated by invaders in the past. Like the Italians — and quite unlike the ancient Romans, therefore — they had developed great skill in dividing themselves rather than others.

Two of Gandhi's earliest schemes for common action that could not easily be transformed into self-divisive action were those which called upon all Indians to spin thread daily, regardless of need and to wear — at least symbolically — garments of homespun cloth. Thus, as Ainslie T. Embree writes,

> the simple white "Gandhi cap" became a symbol of support for the national cause. In a country of extraordinary diversity of dress and manners, the adoption of such an easily recognizable symbol was a stroke of genius, the one thing that high caste and low, rich and poor, the Punjabi, the Madrasi, the Bengali, could use without much difficulty.

Similarly of spinning thread it could be said that, while it "might not do much to alter economic conditions . . . to experience working together . . . gave people an exhilarating sense of participation in the political process."[30] Closely related to these was the program to destroy foreign-made clothes, which drew forth words of reproof from Tagore, as did the companion call to reject all forms of English education till freedom was attained. "Literary training, scholarly research and linguistic pursuits, study of English and Sanskrit and fine arts, had better take a back seat," Gandhi had said, "until at any rate we have won our freedom." ([28] 3) And in an open-letter replying directly to Tagore's criticism on the subject (in *Young India*, October 13, 1921), Gandhi had said with great severity:

> When there is war, the poet lays down the lyre, the lawyer his law reports, the schoolboy his books. The poet will sing the true note after the war is over, the lawyer will have occasion to go to his law books when people have time to fight among themselves. When a house is on fire, all the inmates go out, and each takes up a bucket to quench the fire. When all about me are dying for want of food, the only occupation permissible to me is to feed the hungry. It is my conviction that India is a house on fire because its manhood is being daily scorched, it is dying of hunger because it has no work . . . . At the present moment India has nothing to share with the world save her degradation, pauperism, and plagues . . . . A drowning man cannot save others. In order to be fit to save others, we must try to save ourselves. ([27] 228, 231)

As if to suggest that Bengal's fine literary flowering under British rule, from Carey to Tagore, was rather a burden than an inspiration to him as a nation-builder, Gandhi observed that modern Indian poets "singing hymns of praise" to India "as they soar into the sky" like birds have usually eaten and slept well the night before. "But I have had the pain," he continued, "of watching birds who for want of strength could not be coaxed even to flutter their wings. The human bird under the Indian sky gets up weaker than when he pretended to retire . . . . It is an indescribably painful state which has to be experienced to be realized. I have found it impossible to soothe suffering patients with a song from Kabir" — much less with one from the aristocratic poet laureate of modern India! ([27] 232)

Yet, if it is a time of war, why not simply call upon all Indians to rise up in bloody revolt against their British rulers? Gandhi seemed often on the verge of calling for some such thing. At one painful moment, for example, he had been moved to say: "We shall either free India or die in the attempt; we shall not live to see perpetuation of our slavery."[31] Yet he knew his Indian people, as he knew himself. With terrible candor he therefore said:

> I hold that whatever may be true of other countries, a bloody revolution will not succeed in India. The masses will not respond. And a movement in which masses have no active part can do them no good.... For it would be still foreign rule for them."[32]

His point was that, in the past, when some Indians had risen and fought to seize power, they usually found it easier in the long run to exercise the power they had seized over other Indians, rather than persist in efforts to exercise it over well-trained and united foreigners. They even found it easier to cooperate with such foreigners than to fight them. For that reason there have been historically literally hundreds of independent or semi-independent Indian states, with caste rulers whose attitudes toward their Indian subjects were hardly distinguishable from the attitudes of foreign rulers. On another plane, even the Brahmans had ruled over the Indian social system virtually as conquerors.

Though the ultimate goal was indeed to "do or die" in saying *no* to continued British rule in India, preparation for it on a national scale had to start, according to Gandhi, not with calls to bloody revolt and battle — that was the English way, and the way of some Indians, already accustomed to wearing British uniforms — but with programs of spinning together, wearing homespun cloth, refusing British education, and burning British-made clothes. The underlying spirit would have to be self-sacrificing love. But how best could that spirit be communicated, so that high and low, rich and poor, Muslims and Hindus alike might hear it? Gandhi's answer here has proved to be of incalculable literary-linguistic — as well as political — significance. What speech of India was on a par with spinning thread and wearing *khaddar*? Gandhi's answer was not Bengali or Sanskrit, to be sure, but Hindustani.

Professor Paul R. Brass dwells on the apparent paradox of Gandhi's effort to perfect the communal union of all Hindus and promote the national union of Hindus and Muslims by the same linguistic means. He notes first of all that the Urdu-Hindi divergence, as it developed in the late nineteenth century, had actually served to split the Hindu and Muslim communities *within themselves* as much as it served to set them against one another. In northern India, at any rate, the controversy over the written forms of Hindustani quite obviously had the effect of widening the "divergence between the languages of the educated urban elites and the rural masses, who, Hindus and Muslims alike, spoke a variety of dialects, generically referred to as 'Hindi'." By the time the mass politics of the nationalist era came to the major Hindi-speaking areas in the 1920s, Professor Brass concludes,

> this dual divergence was well advanced and was thus particularly deplored by Gandhi, whose political goals were contrary to both historic tendencies. In the face of Hindu-Muslim divergence, Gandhi favored communal unity; in the face of elite-mass divergence, Gandhi favored mass mobilization. In his writings on language, Gandhi showed an acute awareness of both kinds of divergence and proposed their resolution through the remerging of the two languages, Hindi and Urdu, into the common, everyday language of the masses, which he called Hindustani and which he thought could be written in either script. Gandhi worked through Hindi and Hindustani voluntary associations for the spread of the spoken language, with its fusion of Persian-Arabic, San-

skritic, and indigenous vernacular elements, in the educational institutions of north India and the rest of the country.[33]

To promote Hindustani convincingly, Gandhi made himself a linguist worthy of comparison with Dante. When he first focused his attention on the subject, he accepted the use of the term "Hindi," instead of Hindustani, to designate the hybrid speech that had developed out of the utilitarian intercourse of Hindus and Muslims during the centuries of Muslim rule. His earliest important statement on the subject dates from 1909, when he wrote his highly-influential book on *Indian Home Rule*, later known as *Hind Swaraj*. In that book, which owed so much to Mazzini's ideal of personal self-control as the essence of freedom, Gandhi had written:

> To give millions a knowledge of English is to enslave them . . . . We write to each other in faulty English, and from this even our M.A.s, are not free; our best thoughts are expressed in English; our best newspapers are printed in English. If this state of things continues for a long time, posterity will, it is my firm opinion, condemn and curse us . . . . A universal language for India should be Hindi. ([22] 180)

As Ram Gopal explains in his well-documented though highly partisan book on the *Linguistic Affairs of India* (1966), Gandhi persisted in using "Hindi" for the common spoken language until the early 1920s when, having become linguistically better informed, he switched to the name the Muslims had given it as the speech of the land (Persian *stan*, Sanskrit *sthan*) of the Hindus. ([22] 184) What became obvious to him in the early 1920s was the fact that many Hindu nationalist extremists had already appropriated the term Hindi as their linguistic battle-cry against the last vestiges of Muslim dominance in emancipated Hindu India.

Like Gilchrist long before him, Gandhi regretted that Hindustani had not become for India, under Muslim rule, what heavily-Normanized Anglo-Saxon had become for England in the centuries after 1066. Hindu caste exclusivity had prevented it. But now it was time to make up for past failures by universal acceptance of Hindustani as the name for the speech most widely shared by Indian Muslims and Hindus. That became Gandhi's central line of argument in literally thousands of pages on the theme, only a small portion of which have been collected posthumously in M. K. Gandhi, *Our Language Problem* {Bombay, 1965). Taken together, they are an equivalent of Dante's *De Vulgari Eloquentia* — though the most striking feature throughout is their author's obvious determination not to let five and a half centuries slip by in India, as had happened in Italy, before a political determination of the matter was made.

In this regard, it needs to be stressed that Gandhi's preparation for leadership in India's national independence movement coincided with the period during which the great *Linguistic Survey of India* (11 vols.) was being researched and compiled under the direction of the eminent linguist and literary historian Sir George Abraham Grierson (1851-1941). Lord Macaulay, as already noted, had said in the 1830s that, after the British authorities had produced a new English-educated Indian intellectual elite, it would be the responsibility of that elite, and not of the British, to refine and enrich the regional vernaculars to make them fit vehicles for popular education and, later, for genuine literary development. But, exactly how many regional vernaculars or dialects were there that might profitably be so refined and enriched? That was the last question of high experimental importance for India's linguistic-literary future, to which the British Government of India addressed itself before the Indian "Struggle for Freedom" moved into high gear in the twentieth century. And it was rather definitively answered in Grierson's great survey. Grierson himself, in its early pages,[34] reviewed what earlier scholars had contributed in the field, and his review is thus summed up by Ram Gopal in the introductory pages of his own *Linguistic Affairs of India*:

> Early in the 19th century, the first attempt at a systematic survey of the languages of India was made by William Carey, J. Marshman, and W. Ward . . . . The [resultant] Carey Report contains the names of 33 languages including those of the South, but it regards the latter as being as much Sanskritic as Bengali or Hindi. It was B. H. Hodgson who, some years later (1847), distinguished the Southern languages as a separate family, and used the term "Dravidian" for them. Similarly, in 1854, Max Müller established for the first time the existence of the Munda family of languages as an independent body of speech, apart from the Dravidian. Hodgson's work was carried forward by Bishop Caldwell, who, in his "Comparative Grammar of the Dravidian or South-Indian Family of Languages" (published in 1854), for the first time treated a group of Indian languages as a subject of special study. This was followed by a score of attempts, each making some definite contribution to the . . . basic understanding of the Indian languages. But much yet remained to be done, and this need was emphasized at the Oriental Congress at Vienna in 1886, where the assembled scholars passed a resolution urging the Government of India to undertake "a deliberate systematic survey of the languages of India." ([22] 16)

Grierson himself had been a major proponent of that resolution. And when the British Government of India responded favorably, he was put in charge of the survey. The language inquiry became part of the preparation of the great Census Report of 1901. The Census-takers learned that in many regions the language spoken had never been given a name. People would say of their own mother-tongue, "Oh, that has no name. It is simply correct usage." But those who thus responded would be quick to identify by name several languages at a distance of fifty miles or more, spoken by others. ([22] 16-17) And it was thus that the many, many mother-tongues and dialects of India got all their names registered. Taken as a whole, the Survey is a treasure-house not only of statistics, but also of marvelous insights into how and why certain vernaculars spread and others do not, as also into what becomes of them when religious, ethnic, cultural, or political sectarians attempt to use them in pursuit of non-linguistic ends.

Grierson's *Survey* gives us a linguistic view of India that matches, on a commensurately vaster scale, the view of Italy provided by Dante in the *De Vulgari Eloquentia*. And most striking, finally, are the extraordinary statistical correspondences. Dante begins by inviting his reader to stand with him imaginatively high on the Italian side of the Alps so as to be able to look down the length of the Italian peninsula. The Alps serve Italy as the Himalayas serve India. Viewed imaginatively from a comparable point in the Himalayas, India's main physical divisions would appear to run more or less east and west, setting off the soaring mountain zone of the "Himalaya wheel" in the North, the great Indo-Gangetic plain in the center, and the Peninsula proper extending far to the south. Italy's main physical division, on the contrary, runs in a generally north-south direction, setting off eastern and western halves of the slender peninsula. And "if someone should ask what the line of division is," Dante writes, "I would answer, in a word, the ridge of the Apennines, which, in the manner of a tile roof . . . drains [Italy's] waters into the Tyrrhenian sea on the right and into the Adriatic on the left."

Dante then gives his readers a generalized catalogue of regions and peoples, seven to the west and seven to the east of the Apennines, each with its dominant regional vernacular and related dialects. Starting from the south on the western side there are "Apulia (though not the whole of it), Rome, the Duchy [of Spoleto], Tuscany, and the March of Genoa"; on the eastern side, "the rest of Apulia, the March of Ancona, Romagna, Lombardy, and the March of Treviso with Venetia." That gives five on each side. He then assigns the islands of the Tyrrhenian sea, Sicily and Sardinia, to the western side, and the regions of Friuli and Istria to the eastern. North and south, east and west, the peoples of all these regions, Dante stresses, speak different languages. And Dante here gives us this extraordinary paragraph which, simply with the substitution of Indian for the Italian names of places and peoples, could stand as a statistically accurate summation of the Grierson Survey as updated in the more recent census reports:

> From this it appears that Italy alone is divided into at least fourteen vernaculars. And all of these vernaculars are further divided within themselves, so that in Tuscany, for instance, the language of the Sienese differs from that of the Arezzi, and in Lombardy, that of Ferrara from that of Piacentia. And we may even observe certain differences within a single city, as I remarked above. And so if I were to add up the primary, secondary, and subsidiary differences in the vernaculars of Italy, I would not just approach a figure like one thousand different dialects in this, the smallest corner of the world, but would even exceed this figure. ([1] 16-17)

Grierson's statistics are conveniently summarized and discussed in the opening paragraphs of Suniti Kumar Chatterji's article of the late 1950s — which, to stress its link with Grierson's work, he titled "Linguistic Survey of India: Languages and Scripts" — contributed to S. Radhakrishnan's *The Cultural Heritage of India* (Vol. I, 1958). Professor Chatterji there writes: "The meticulous and all-inclusive classification of the languages and dialects current in India . . . as given in the *Linguistic Survey of India*, shows a total number of 179 languages and 544 dialects." In a footnote he observed that the figures of the 1951 census raised the total to 845, and we may add that subsequent counts have not only approached a figure like one thousand, as Dante says, but exceeded it. "These figures," Chatterji continues,

> are staggering indeed for any single country or State claiming to be a nation, but they are to be taken with

some caution and reservation .... [In fact] the consideration of dialects is irrelevant when we mention the languages to which they belong, for it is the great literary languages that really matter."[35]

Already the Constitution of the Union of India that went into effect on January 26, 1950 had identified in its much-debated Schedule Eight precisely fourteen "languages of India" that qualified officially as literary languages. The fourteen included Sanskrit and thirteen vernaculars. In the 1960s after much more debate, a fourteenth vernacular was added to the list, completing the parallel with Dante's "at least fourteen." Chatterji is prepared to admit one other, the language of neighboring Nepal; and he therefore concludes that, at the very most,

considering all these matters, it will be seen that India has only the following fifteen great literary languages: (1) Hindi and (2) Urdu, which are but two styles of the same Hindustani speech, employing two totally different scripts and borrowing words from two different sources, (3) Bengali, (4) Assamese, (5) Oriya, (6) Marathi, (7) Gujarati, (8) Sindhi, (9) Punjabi, (10) Kashmiri, (11) Nepali, (12) Telugu, (13) Kannada, (14) Tamil, and (15) Malayalam. ([35] 53-54)

Gandhi's attitude toward the fourteen or fifteen chief regional languages of India was substantially the same as Dante's toward those of Italy. As a nation-builder, Gandhi quickly recognized the importance of the regions of India to the Indian nationalist movement which, he said, could not conceivably succeed if what he called the "Congress 'national' middle class shell" could not be quickly filled with genuine national life by "drawing in regional blood." As Karat Prakash observes in *Language and Nationality Politics in India* (1973), "Gandhi's success in this respect is reflected in his approach to the Indian languages. Gandhi was one of the few Congress leaders to consistently study the linguistic question."[36] Basically, Gandhi agreed wholly with Dante's view that, regardless of their numbers, the naturally-acquired mother-tongues or dialects were to be preferred to any grammatically-formalized secondary language "learned by the rules" in school. Some of the Italian regional languages, in Dante's view, had already taken great strides toward the common goal. He had in fact said:

> I readily agree with those who place the Bolognese first among the vernacular languages, considering them only in relation to the other municipal languages of Italy. But if they, on the other hand, think that the vernacular of Bologna is to be preferred in an absolute sense, I disagree with them strongly.

Granting that, as now developed, it had *some* of the requirements of a truly national literary language, it did not, he insisted, as yet have enough of them to end the regional competition; otherwise, he had very pointedly added, the best "poets of Bologna, such as the superlative Guido Guinizelli, or Guido Ghislieri, or Fabruzzo, or Onesto, or the others, would never have departed from their own vernacular," making increasing use of words and constructions, as Dante illustrates, that "are absolutely different from those of the inhabitants of the center of Bologna," and that obviously tended, like Dante's own departures from Florentine, toward a common higher form. ([1] 26-27)

  Of course, while the regional dialects of Italy were developing themselves organically toward a common higher form, the traditional Latin of the Church remained available for transregional and international use. Dante had no objection to its continued use in that capacity. In Gandhi's India, English was the obvious equivalent of Church Latin. If Gandhi could have brought himself to tolerate its continued service in that capacity — as it came in fact to be tolerated immediately alter his death — the linguistic situations of India in the twentieth century and of Italy in the thirteenth would have been identical. But Gandhi was, as we have seen, absolutely determined to break with English.

And it was that determination that forced him into what can only be described as a tragic linguistic dilemma. As Professsor Prakash sums up the Mahatma's language "priorities" right down to the time of his assassination in 1948:

> He first of all decided that English dominance was harmful for all linguistic groups in India. Thereby he set a common task for all Indians — the removal of the ruler's tongue, which did "violence" to the manhood of Indians . . . . Next he advocated the substitution of Hindustani as the lingua franca. . . . Both the Hindus and the Muslims, the two major communities of India, were to find a common identity in this colloquial tongue . . . . In doing so, Gandhi hoped that Hindustani would find acceptance in the South. He was mistaken. . . . Given the importance of the Hindu-Muslim conflict and the Ganges belt during the height of the independence struggle, Gandhi overlooked the divisions among the Hindus . . . . However, Gandhi adhered to the principle of linguistic states and consistently put forward the proposal of linguistic reorganization of the provinces as beneficial for an independent India. As for the regional languages, he said: "The redistribution of provinces on a linguistic basis is necessary if provincial languages are to grow to their full height. Hindustani has to be the lingua franca, the Rashtra Bhasha of India, but it cannot take the place of the provincial tongues. It cannot be the medium of instruction — much less English." Gandhi understood the vital role of the mother-tongue, despite his awareness of the need for an all-India language. ([36] 155-156)

Back in 1917, when he first began to discuss publicly "which Indian language should be the national language," Gandhi was full of hope that he could persuade his fellow nationalists, North and South, East and West — Muslims as well as Hindus, Dravidian-language users as well as Aryan-language users — to move along with him toward a common goal. His proposals at the Gujarati Education Conference convened in Broach on October 20, 1917, for instance, read like they could have been paraphrased out of the most reasonably argued sections of Dante's *De Vulgari Eloquentia*. To his Gujarati-speaking audience he says at one point, "Let us see what should be the requirements of a national language," and then he proceeds to spell out his notion of them as follows:

1. It should be easy to learn for Government officials.
2. It should be capable of serving as a medium of religious, economic, and political intercourse throughout India.
3. It should be the speech of the majority of the inhabitants of India.
4. It should be easy to learn for the whole of the country.
5. In choosing this language, considerations of temporary or passing interest should not count. ([22] 180)

Discounting the fifth requirement as essentially non-linguistic- — being rather a call for "fair play" on the part of advocates — we can say that, in the corresponding passage of his *De Vulgari Eloquentia*, ([1] 28-31) Dante gives us a comparable list of four requirements, against which, as he says, all the vernaculars "are to be measured, weighed, and compared." The truly eloquent vernacular we are searching for, he says, must be *illustre* (illustrious), *cardinale* (cardinal), *aulicum* (courtly), and *curiale* (curial). Although the English cognates provided in parentheses hardly suffice to indicate Dante's understanding of the Latin terms, they are obviously, in Latin, high-sounding epithets that might well have delighted the old high-caste guardians of the purity of classical Sanskrit, and perhaps many of the modern cultivators of Carey's Sanskritized Bengali as opposed to Gilchrist's hybrid Hindustani of the camp-followers.

Dante proceeds to explain each of his four requirements at some length, supplying examples to clarify the meaning where necessary. "Illustrious," as he uses the term, means both "luminous" in itself and capable of "spreading its light," of illuminating others. In a language of literary eloquence, the quality manifests its presence as a form of exaltation shared by those who speak and write it and those who hear and read it. In Gandhi's list of requirements, it corresponds to requirement 2, the capacity of a language to serve as a medium for intercourse on the highest possible cultural level. "Cardinal," taking it in its basic etymological sense, means capable of serving as a great hinge on which all the other vernaculars and dialects of a country necessarily turn, so that all tend to become more and more like it as it carries them around. In Gandhi's list, it corresponds to the requirement that a national language ought to become, if it is not already, the speech of a majority of the country's inhabitants.

The terms "courtly" and "curial" are related terms. As Dante explains it, "courtly" means that the language sought must be such that, "if we Italians had a royal court," which is to say a central seat of government, like France or England, "this vernacular would be "spoken in the palace." It corresponds to Gandhi's first requirement, that a national language should be "easy to learn for government officials." "Curial" means worthy of use in a country's courts of law, where citizens come to get "fair treatment" under the law. The language Dante is after must be one that gives all who willingly consent to its national use their "due," or justice. It must not be hard on some and easy on others. On Gandhi's list, the equivalent is requirement four, that the language should be "easy to learn for the whole country."

Which of the Italian vernaculars qualifies as illustrious, cardinal, courtly, and curial in the senses defined? None, says Dante, though the practice of the best writers in several of them points them in the right direction. By the time he has completed his *Commedia*, Dante will have his answer. He will know that, by building on the labors of other vernacular poets, and training himself to do poetic justice to a form of love dictating in his heart which was unknown to the ancients, he had himself fashioned the required language. Yet, as already indicated, it would take over five and a half centuries before Italy ceased to be but a geographical expression, to become a truly unified nation with a centralized government, or "royal court," and a national system of justice. One of the more moving passages of Dante's *De Vulgari Eloquentia* expresses an attitude and mood which we often find expressed in books about the divided condition of India before 1947. Italy, Dante says, has indeed no centralized system of justice (curia), but it has the components of such a system, for there is a sense of cultural unity pervading its many regions despite their political fragmentation. That is what permits him to affirm that, when the longed-for language that is illustrious, cardinal, and courtly finally makes its appearance, it will be fairly judged — fairly weighed in the balance — in the various regions. The point is, he concludes, that, just as members of a functioning national system of justice with courtrooms located throughout the land "are unified by a single sovereign," so the members of this emergent national language we are seeking "are unified by the grace of a divine intellectual light. For this reason, although we lack a single sovereign, it would be false to say that we lack an Italian system of dispensing justice (*curia*): we do have such a system, although the members of its body are scattered around."

That tribunal capable of weighing the literary achievements in the various Italian vernaculars is what Professor Devoto will refer to as the scattered elites of "letterati" who will cherish and develop Dante's language through the centuries of Italian political disunity, until they can finally turn it over to the centralized government that Mazzini, Cavour, and Garibaldi will bring into being late in the nineteenth century. As R. C. Majumdar writes at the close of his chapter on the "Indian People at the Beginning of the Nineteenth Century," at that time "the whole country was divided into a very large number of self-contained units, almost mutually exclusive in character, and the conception of India as a common motherland was still in the realm of fancy. There was no India as it is understood today. There were Bengalis, Hindusthanis, Marathas, Sikhs, etc., but no Indians, at the beginning of the nineteenth century. There was, however, a complete revolution of ideas at the end of the century. One who speaks of an Indian nation at the beginning of the nineteenth century does as much violence to historical facts as those who refuse to recognize it at the end of that century." ([20] 28-29)

But, as we have already indicated, if India in 1900 had advanced linguistically to the point where Italy was in 1300, pairing Tagore with the young Dante, there is the all-important difference that India after 1900 was not to have to wait five and a half centuries for its equivalent of Mazzini, Cavour, and Garibaldi. Gandhi comes fast on the heels of Tagore. And Gandhi has an absolute impatience with the idea of leaving it to scattered elites of "letterati" to decide a question of such overriding importance to him as that of united independent India's national language. Thus, after having spelled out the requirements of a national language before his Gujarati audience in 1917, the Mahatma asks abruptly, "Which is the language that fulfils these requirements?" And he proceeds to answer without hesitation that only two of India's vernaculars could possibly qualify. And they are, of course, the same two that John Gilchrist and William Carey had fought for over a century before: Hindustani (now long since polarized, however, into literary High Hindi and High Urdu) and Bengali. Of the two, says Gandhi, Hindustani as spoken is obviously more widely used, since even Bengalis themselves "make use of it outside Bengal," whereas the Hindi-Hindustani speaker persists in speaking in his own language "wherever he goes and no one is surprised at this." Using the terms Hindi and Urdu as constituents of the single Hindustani speech, Gandhi continues:

> The Hindi-speaking Hindu preachers and the Urdu-speaking Maulvis make their religious speeches through-

out India in Hindi and Urdu and even the illiterate masses understand them. Even an unlettered Gujarati, when he goes to the North attempts to speak a few Hindi words. But the Northern bhaiya [brother] who works as gate-keeper to the Bombay seth [big business man] declines to speak in Gujarati and it is the seth, his employer who is obliged to speak to him in broken Hindi. I have heard Hindi [Hindustani] spoken even in far off southern provinces. It is not correct to say that in Madras one cannot do without English. I have successfully used Hindi [Hindustani] there for all my work. In the trains I have heard Madrasi passengers speaking to other passengers in Hindi. Besides . . . it has to be noted that Muslims throughout India speak Urdu and they are found in large numbers in every province. Thus Hindi [the Hindustani hybrid *lingua franca*] has already established itself as the national language of India. We have been using it as such for a long time. ([22] 181)

Who is it among the Hindu Indians, Gandhi then asks, that finds it too difficult to learn Hindustani, or refuses to learn it for reasons of cultural pride? Gandhi's reply here recalls some of Dante's caustic judgments about speakers of the more and less sophisticated vernaculars of Italy, particularly the Sardinians and Romans. To learn Hindustani, Gandhi writes,

no doubt presents some difficulty to the educated classes of Madras . . . . It is not easy for Tamilians. Tamil and other languages of the South belong to the Dravidian group. Their structure and grammar are different from those of Sanskrit. The only thing common between these two groups is their Sanskrit vocabulary. But the difficulty is confined to the present educated classes only." ([22] 181-182)

In the past, educated Dravidian-language speakers of the South had always preferred to study Sanskrit itself, as the sacred language of Hinduism, rather than any modern Aryan vernacular that brought with it no significant literary culture. Against that attitude, Gandhi urged that he had a "right to appeal to their patriotic spirit and expect them to put forth a special effort" to learn Hindustani.

By way of transition to a discussion of the attitude of the Bengali, Gandhi then says: "Bengal and Madras are the two provinces that are cut off from the rest of India for want of knowledge of Hindustani on their part, Bengal, because of its prejudice against learning any other language of India, and Madras, because of the difficulty of the Dravidians about picking up Hindustani. An average Bengali can learn Hindustani in two months if he gave it three hours per day and Dravidian in six months at the same rate. Neither a Bengali nor a Dravidian can hope to achieve the same result with English in the same time." The Bengali prejudice, he quickly adds, extends also to the matter of scripts. It was Gandhi's belief that, if it were "possible to adopt a common script, we should remove a great hindrance in the way of realizing the dream, which at present is, of having a common language." The Indian Muslims who had done so for centuries, he often said, were justified in continuing to write Hindustani in the Perso-Arabic script. But what is the possible use, he would complain, of having so many different scripts for the Aryan and heavily Sanskritized vernaculars used only by Hindus? That question gives Gandhi an opportunity for a blistering tirade against the cultural pride or vainglory of Tagore's compatriots of Bengal who seemed to be as jealously protective of their literary language as the old Brahman pandits had been of their sacred Sanskrit texts. In Gandhi's words:

> The Aryan languages have so much in common that, if a great deal of time had not to be wasted in mastering the different scripts, we should all know several languages without much difficulty; for instance, most people who have a little knowledge of Sanskrit would have no difficulty in understanding the matchless creation of Rabindranath Tagore, if it was all printed in Devanagari script. But the Bengali script is a notice to the non-

Bengalis — "hands off." Conversely, if the Bengalis knew the Devanagari script, they would at once be able to enjoy the marvelous beauty and spirituality of Tulsidas, and a host of Hindustani writers . . . . A common script for all of India is a distant ideal. A common script for all those who speak the Indo-Sanskrit languages, including the Southern stock, is a practical ideal, if we but shed our provincialism . . . . That the Devanagari script should be the common script, I suppose, does not need any demonstration — the deciding factor being that it is the script known to the largest part of India. ([22] 183-184)

Gandhi was of course fully aware of the fact that for a long time Bengali nationalist leaders had supported the use of Hindustani as an all-India *lingua franca* to replace English. In fact, in 1925 he had succeeded with relatively little difficulty in getting the Indian National Congress to adopt his position on Hindustani to the point of amending its constitution to read:

> The proceedings of the Congress shall be conducted as far as possible in Hindustani. The English language or any provincial language may be used if the speaker is unable to speak Hindustani. Proceedings of the Provincial Congress Committees shall ordinarily be conducted in the language of the province concerned. Hindustani may also be used. ([22] 187)

Some say that Gandhi "bullied" the Congress leaders into accepting his view of the language question, against their own politically sounder judgments. And that seems to have been borne out by the increasing divergence of many leaders from his view once it became clear that the British would "quit India" before long, thus removing the main argument for replacement of English as quickly as possible with a native all-India language. Gandhi, however, continued his virtually irresistible moral pressure right down to the eve of partition and independence in 1947 and beyond. As Professor Panikkar has put it:

> The dominance of Mahatma Gandhi in the political life

of India for over twenty-five years had held in check the forces of Hindu communalism. With him Hindu-Muslim unity, which in effect meant the support of the claims of the Muslims for social consideration, was a fundamental political principle. But with the approach of Independence those who claimed a dominant position for the Hindus and the creation of a Hindu state in India began to gain strength, especially as it became clear that the Muslims were determined to create a homeland for themselves. If Pakistan was to be created as a homeland for the Muslims of India, why should not the rest be converted into a Hindustan; so the argument ran.[37]

Gandhi never wavered, however. Just a few days before Independence, he was thus passionately scolding his peers: "The Congress must stand like a rock. It dare not give way on the *lingua franca* of India. It cannot be Persianized Urdu or Sanskritized Hindi. It must be a beautiful blend of the two simple forms written in either script. Let us not turn away from the Urdu script."[38]

After partition and independence, with the British gone and a majority of India's Muslims off on their own, the centrifugal forces that Gandhi had held in check seemed on the verge of ripping even the Hindu Indian community apart. On the linguistic level, the Dravidians began to voice strong objection to any form of Aryan linguistic dominance in the South, while among the Aryan-language speakers, the literarily advanced regions increasingly objected to the idea of hurriedly replacing their languages with "humble Hindi," much less with hybrid Hindustani. Shortly before his death, Gandhi acknowledged that he had been sharply pained by the rejection of so much of his design for India's national integration. He said "it was indeed true that he had all along labored under an illusion." Yet he added quickly that he "was never sorry for it," since he "realized that if his vision had not been clouded by that illusion, India would never have reached the point which it had done today." ([32] 295) Was the partition of British India a total failure? A United India would have been preferable, to be sure. But under what conditions could it have been realized?

According to Gandhi, the relation between the majority community of India's Hindus (who were formerly subjects) and the minority community of her Muslims (who were formerly rulers) could hardly lend itself to simple solutions. Is political unity of a voluntary kind so much as imaginable between two such communities? In answer to that question, "I would say the same thing now," wrote Gandhi on the eve of partition, "that I used to say back in 1921, namely, that voluntary surrender on the part of either community, preferably the majority community, of all rights and privileges would immediately effect this unity." What he apparently had in mind was something like what the Norman rulers in England did by adopting the national name and language of their English subjects. The Muslims in India had failed to do the same when they ruled largely because the Hindu caste-system prevented it; but now, in the twentieth century, as he put it: "It would be a great thing, a brave thing, for Hindus to achieve this act of self-denial. Let them say to the Musalmans, 'Have as big a share of the spoils as you want, we will be content to serve you.' . . . It is this spirit of service which I want to permeate the atmosphere. I want you to join me and share this aspiration . . . . I have no other secret but that of voluntary surrender." ([28] 61)

How far was Gandhi, as a practical nation-builder, really prepared to go with that sort of *noblesse oblige* assignment for the Hindu majority of modern India? In April 1947, when Lord Mountbatten was attempting to negotiate a last minute agreement between Muhammed Ali Jinnah, head of the Indian Muslim League, and the Indian National Congress leaders, Gandhi actually advanced a plan for "solving the Indian deadlock" by means of such a Hindu unilateral sacrifice of interests. As B. N. Pandy represents the plan in *The Break-up of British India* (1969):

It was nothing less "than to dismiss the present cabinet [dominated by Hindus] and call on Jinnah to appoint an all-Muslim administration." Gandhi promised to persuade Congress to accept this plan. As it turned out Congress did not accept the plan and Gandhi withdrew it.[39]

It needs to be stressed at this point that Gandhi's insistence on the name Hindustani for the proposed all-India national language was really an integral part of his design for unity through voluntary surrender — if not of real interests, like the reins of government, at least of symbols. As Donald Eugene Smith explains in *India as a Secular State* (1963):

> The significance of the name "Hindustani," and the reason for Gandhi's desire to have it recognized as the official language, was that it was a living spoken language which expressed the cultural synthesis which had already taken place in north India. The natural process by which a Sanskrit-derived language had assimilated Persian and Arabic expressions over a period of hundreds of years was recognized in the name "Hindustani." As Maulan Azad explained to the Constituent Assembly: "by adopting the name Hindustani, the Congress had recognized that natural law by which languages evolve." The use of the term "Hindi" suggests a different kind of development, with emphasis on the literary language which has drawn heavily on Sanskrit. ([38} 400)

There is another side to the coin, however; and Jawaharlal Nehru supplies it in his *Discovery of India*. "The correct word for Indian, as applied to country or culture or the historical continuity of our varying traditions," he explains there, "is 'Hindi' from 'Hind,' a shortened form of Hindustan.... In the countries of Western Asia, in Iran and Turkey, in Iraq, Afghanistan, Egypt, and elsewhere, India has always been referred to as, and is still called, Hind; and everything Indian is called Hindi." Nehru notes that "Americans who call all Indians Hindus are not far wrong," although it would be preferable if they used the term Hindi. Then he concludes:

> Unfortunately the word Hindi has become associated in India with a particular script — the Devanagari script of Sanskrit — and so it has become difficult to use it in its larger and more natural significance. Perhaps when present-day controversies subside we may revert to its original and more satisfying use. Today the word Hindustani is used for Indian; it is of course derived from Hindustan. But this is too much of a mouthful and it has no such historical and cultural associations as Hindi has. It would certainly appear odd to refer to ancient periods of Indian culture as "Hindustani." ([8] 65)

*4. Conclusion: Literary India Today*

Perhaps it was simply one of those notorious "right mistakes" of Gandhi to have insisted on "Hindustani in two scripts" as the Indian national language right down through the time of partition and beyond. Perhaps it was necessary to "divide and conquer" the problem of India's Muslim and Hindu communities — her "two eyes," as they have been called — so as to afford each of them the experience of minority as well as majority status in an independent Indian state. After partition, Gandhi devoted the rest of his life to "fighting" for Muslim minority rights in the preponderantly Hindu Union of India and for Hindu minority rights in Pakistan. He insisted, in the last year of his life, that "India and Pakistan were to be reunited, in spirit if not in a technical sense," and "spoke of his eagerness to go to Pakistan to ease the communal tensions there as he had done in India"; he "confronted urban communal violence in Calcutta and Delhi and everywhere struggled to control the growing hatred between India and Pakistan." ([38] 295)

On the level of language, it is certainly true that, as Professor Prakash says, during the meetings of the Constituent Assembly charged with drawing up the Constitution of the Union of India that went into effect on January 26, 1950 — which is to say, during the period 1948-1950 immediately following Gandhi's death — "Hindustani, the Gandhian instrument of communal bridge-building, was unceremoniously jettisoned," and that the Constitution then framed "neglected to define the scope and role of the fourteen national languages" listed in its Eighth Schedule. ([36] 157) Yet, in retrospect, a more careful reading of the two chief articles of that Constitution that have to do with the "official language" and its cultivation into a "national literary language" reveals them to be permeated with the Gandhian national spirit. Article 343 made "Hindi in the Devanagari script," not Hindustani in both scripts, the "official language of the Union." ([22] 192) But it also very prudently provided that there would be a delay of fifteen years before any effort would be made to substitute Hindi for English as the all-India language where there was any objection to it; and when that moratorium actually expired in 1965, it was indefinitely extended because of strong pressure in the Dravidian language areas especially but also among the Bengali and speakers of some of the other "more sophisticated" Aryan languages. When Indira Gandhi was defeated by a Hindu-Hindi nationalist coalition in 1977, it appeared for a time that a strenuous effort might be made to "impose" Hindi. But, before long, the daughter of Jawaharlal Nehru was swept back into office by a landslide electoral margin that appeared to have put an end to any idea of actually displacing English with Hindi in the foreseeable future.

But the more important language provision of the 1950 Constitution is contained in article 351, which reads: "it shall be the duty of the Union to promote the spread of the Hindi language, to develop it so that it may serve as a medium of expression for all the elements of the composite culture of India and to secure its enrichment by assimilating without interfering with its genius, the forms, styles and expressions used in Hindustani and in the other languages of India specified in the Eighth Schedule, and by drawing, wherever necessary or desirable, for its vocabulary, primarily on Sanskrit and secondarily on other languages." ([22] 193-194) The phrasing of that article — which echoes Dante's criteria for eloquence in a vernacular as well as Gandhi's requirements for a national language — is surely a masterpiece of philological diplomacy. There is no pretense in the article that the perfection of Hindi is already in any sense an accomplished fact; and the continuance of English as an alternate "official language" serves to emphasize that Hindi has a long way to go before its status as an all-India literary language can be substantially advanced by governmental means. In fact, as Professor Prakash notes, the chief champions of Hindi are becoming increasingly aware that, unless Hindi allies itself with the other regional languages, encouraging the development of all equally, it stands very little chance of ever displacing English as the all-India language. Profesor Prakash writes:

> The key to Hindi, or the future of India's Official Language, which will be the all-India medium, rests with the regional languages, i.e. the language of the center is dependent on the languages of the state.... In practice, this would mean the encouraging of the state languages. The time taken for these languages to play their normal role would give Hindi scope to develop and when the time comes for the switch there would be no vested interests in favor of English. [The meaning here is that "Hindi should join the forces it cannot beat," making common cause with the regional languages generally in trying to displace English in the states.] Time will determine the solution. However, this might be too optimistic a forecast. Hindi would still be suspect in the non-Hindi areas as a northern language out to dominate. But there are sufficient grounds to hope that once the regional languages have grown to their full stature, they can accept Hindi on equal terms. ([36] 170-171)

The question that immediately suggests itself is this:

Is English destined to wither away and die in India as the regional languages, accepting Hindi on equal terms, grow to full stature? Most modern historians and literary critics seem to think it a very unlikely prospect. Professor Panikkar, for instance, holds rather that by "ceasing to be the language of the conqueror," English is "likely to be naturalized more easily as one of the languages of India as Persian was for over 400 years. Indo-Persian, during its 400 years of existence in India, developed an independent literature, and the language itself is still part of Indian tradition. A similar development of English is not only possible but probable, more especially because, as the most widely used international language, its cultivation will continue to be of the highest importance to India itself." ([37] 138) Sir Percival Spear, too, has observed that "culturally the English language has been reprieved, now that there is no political opponent to be annoyed by abolishing it." ([4] 348-349) Krishna Kripalani reminds us that English remains a "link" language "among the intelligentsia all over India," even as it was when Nehru, as Prime Minister of India, was able to communicate with India's President, Dr. S. Radhakrishnan, only in English; and also that the chief edition of Gandhi's works is in English, as is the original text of the Union Constitution. ([4] 419-420)

But apart from the obvious utilitarian value of English, there is the fact that, from the days of Rammohun Roy to the present, many distinguished Indian writers have chosen to use the English language, sometimes even to pursue a genuinely Indian literary fame in it. Professor Buitenen has observed that, in this regard, the English "language and the literary values it embodies are today vital forces as well as matters of controversy" in India. "Many writers," he adds, insist that they "can write creatively only in Bengali or Marathi or Tamil or whatever their native language, though they might be bilingual in that language and in English"; other writers insist "that English is as native to them as any other language" — which has led one recent sage (as the editors of *The Literatures of India: An Introduction* note) to conclude that "Indian writing is what is written by Indians" regardless of language. ([2] 5, 6, 240)

Thus for the modern vernacular languages of India taken together, with English among them, it may be said that they are now quite obviously in free competition for literary primacy, and that the "ground-rules" for their competition are virtually identical with those recommended by Dante in his *De Vulgari Eloquentia*. And it may be that they will finally enjoy many centuries of such competition before a Dante emerges among them who can command the absolute approval and acceptance of all his fellow writers in the vernaculars as India's truly national poet. India's next equivalent of Dante will surely not write his masterpiece in English — Gandhi's spirit would never allow it; yet it is likely that, whatever his native regional language, he is apt to know English, too, at least as well as Dante knew the supra-regional language of his day in which he wrote his treatise on eloquence in the vernacular.

NOTES

*After the first numbered reference to sources identified in the notes below, subsequent references appear parenthetically in the text with the note-number in square brackets followed by the page ([n#] p.).

1. Robert S. Haller, ed., *Literary Criticism of Dante Alighieri*, University of Nebraska Press, Lincoln, 1973, pp. 4-5. Although the page references here and in subsequent citations of *Dante's On Eloquence* in the Vernacular are to Haller's volume, in many instances the translations have been slightly modified, always in accordance with the Latin text of the *De Vulgari Eloquentia*, ed. by Aristide Marigo, Felice le Monnier, Firenze, 1957.

2. Edward C. Dimock, Jr., Edwin Gerow, C. M. Naim, A. K. Ramanujan, Gordon Roadarmel, J. A. B. van Buitenen, *The Literatures of India: An Introduction*, University of Chicago Press, Chicago, 1974, p. 13.

3. Clarence Maloney, "The Real Language Problem in South Asia," in *Asian Affairs*, 5, May-June 1974, 320-321.

4. T. Burrow, "Ancient and Modern Languages," in *A Cultural History of India*, A. L. Basham, ed., Clarendon Press, Oxford, 1975, p. 162.

5. *Hegel: On the Arts*, abridged and trans. by H. Paolucci, 2nd ed.,Griffon House Publications [for the Bagehot Council], Smyrna, Delaware, 2001, p. 155.

6. In G. T. Garratt, ed., *The Legacy of India*, Clarendon Press, Oxford, 1937, p. 67.

7. Percival Spear, *India, Pakistan, and the West*, 4th ed., Oxford University Press, Oxford, 1967, pp. 24-25.

8. Jawaharlal Nehru, *The Discovery of India*, John Day Company, New York, 1946, pp. 158-159.

9. Erich Auerbach, *Introduction to Romance Languages and Literature*, Capricorn Books, New York, 1961, p. 131.

10. Giacomo Devoto, *The Languages of Italy*, trans. by V. Louise Katainen, University of Chicago Press, Chicago, 1978, p. 146.

11. Thomas A. Sebeok, ed., *Portraits of Linguists*, Indiana University Press, Bloomington, 1967, Vol. I, pp. 5-6.

12. L. S. S. O'Malley, ed., *Modern India and the West*, Oxford University Press, Oxford, 1941, p. 225.

13. David Kopf, *British Orientalism and the Bengal Renaissance: The Dynamics of Indian Modernization 1773-1835*, University of California Press, Berkeley, 1969, pp. 89-90.

14. George Smith, *The Life of William Carey*, J. M. Dent, London, 1885, p. 167.

15. J. C. Ghosh, *Bengali Literature*, Oxford University Press, Oxford, 1948, p. 112.

16. T. B. Macaulay, *Selected Writings*, University of Chicago Press, Chicago, 1972, p.249.

17. Louis H. Gray, *Foundations of Language*, Macmillan, New York, 1939, p. 441.

18. R. H. Robins, *A Short History of Linguistics*, Indiana University Press, Bloomington, 1967.

19. Humayun Kabir, *Studies in Bengali Poetry*, BharatiyaVidya Bhavan, Bombay, 1962, pp. 70-76.

20. R. C. Majumdar, ed., *History and Culture of the Indian People*, 11 vols., Bharatiya Vidya Bhavan, Bombay, 1951-1977; Vol. 10, *British Paramountcy and Indian Renaissance, Part II*, 1965, p. 219.

21. T. W. Clark, *The Novel in India*, University of Chicago Press, Chicago, 1970, p. 146.

22. Ram Gopal, *Linguistic Affairs of India*, Asia Publishing House, Bombay, 1966, pp. 46-47.

23. Dino Bigongiari, *Essays on Dante and Medieval Culture*, H. Paolucci, ed., 2nd ed., Griffon House Publications [for the Bagehot Council], Smyrna, Delaware, 2000, pp. 47-63.

24. Percival Spear, *Oxford History of Modem India*, Clarendon Press, Oxford, 1965, p. 333.

25. Herbert H. Gowen, *A History of Indian Literature*, Appleton, New York, 1931, pp. 9, 10.

26. A. Gupta, ed. *Studies in the Bengal Renaissance*, Council of Education, Calcutta, 1958, pp. 268-269.

27. Homer A. Jack, *The Gandhi Reader*, Indiana University Press, Bloomington, 1956, p. 222.

28. D. G. Tendulkar, *Mahatma*, Government of India, Delhi, 1961, III, p. 234.

29. C. D. S. Devanesen, *Making of the Mahatma*, Orient Longmans, Madras, 1969, pp. 332, 334.

30. A. T. Embree, *India's Search for National Identity*, Knopf, New York, 1972, p. 77.

31. D. G. Tendulkar, *Mahatma*, Government of India, Delhi, 1962, VI, p. 161.

32. F. G. Hutchins, *India's Revolution*, Harvard University Press, Cambridge, 1973, p. 202.

33. P. R. Brass, *Language, Religion, and Politics in Northern India*, Cambridge University Press, Cambridge, 1974, pp. 134-135.

34. G. A. Grierson, ed., *Linguistic Survey of India*, 11 vols., Gov. of India, Calcutta, 1903-1928, 1,11-12.

35. S. Radhakrishnan, *Cultural Heritage of India*, Ramakrishna Mission, Calcutta, I. p. 53.

36. K. Prakash, *Language and Nationality Politics*, Orient Longmans, Madras, 1973, p. 155.

37. K. M. Panikkar, *Foundations of New India*, Allen and Unwin, London, 1963, p.249.

38. D. S. Smith, *India as a Secular State*, Princeton University Press, Princeton, 1967, p. 399.

39. B. N. Pandey, *The Break-up of British India*, Macmillan, London, 1969, p.194.